W9-ARU-679

Betty Crocker
quick
fixes

100 Recipes for the Way You Really Cook

1807 WILEY 2007

Wiley Publishing, Inc.

Library of Congress Cataloging-in-Publication Data:
Betty Crocker quick fixes : 100 recipes for the way you really cook.
    p. cm.
  Includes index.
  ISBN 978-0-470-17352-7 (cloth)
  1. Quick and easy cookery. I. Crocker, Betty. II. Title: Quick fixes.
  TX833.5.B48835 2007
  641.5'55—dc22

                    2007013683

General Mills

Directors, Book and Online Publishing:
Maggie Gilbert and Lynn Vettel

Manager, Cookbook Publishing:
Lois Tlusty

Recipe Development and Testing:
Betty Crocker Kitchens

Photography and Food Styling: General Mills
Photography Studios and Image Library

Wiley Publishing, Inc.

Publisher: Natalie Chapman

Executive Editor: Anne Ficklen

Project Editor: Adam Kowit

Editor: Lauren Brown

Production Manager: Leslie Anglin

Cover Design: Suzanne Sunwoo

Art Director: Tai Blanche

Layout: Indianapolis Composition Services

Manufacturing Manager: Kevin Watt

Manufactured in China

10 9 8 7 6 5 4 3 2 1

Wiley Anniversary Logo: Richard J. Pacifico

Cover photo: Southwestern Chicken Scaloppine
(page 57)

Our Betty Crocker Kitchens seal guarantees success in your kitchen. Every recipe has been tested in America's Most Trusted Kitchens™ to meet our high standards of reliability, easy preparation and great taste.

Dear Friends,

You're hungry . . . but there's so little time to cook. Instead of grabbing a handful of potato chips or bowl of cereal, think about preparing a quick salad, a pasta dish or a super-fast fillet of fish. Think tasty, healthy, easy and filling.

Discover Quick Fixes. Each recipe goes from shopping bag to table in 30 minutes or less. You'll find a range of dinner options from hearty burgers and beer-battered fish to light main-dish salads. Spice up your weekly routine with speedy specialties from the Mexican Night chapter. Or go meatless with tasty dishes like Chunky Vegetable Chili.

These recipes have little to no preparation, cook quickly and serve faster than you can imagine. Now you have more time to enjoy it all.

Enjoy!

Betty Crocker

contents

Fast Eats

Fast food doesn't have to be second rate . . . not if you cook the Betty way! You can enjoy homemade, fabulous food every day — and still spend only minutes in the kitchen. The secret? Foods with built-in convenience and Betty's fast-to-fix ideas.

Let Someone Else Do the Work!

For good food real fast, rely on your butcher, the folks at your fish market or your grocer to short-cut cooking time for you. It's all in what you purchase. Fill your shopping basket with some of these items and see how much faster "homecooked" becomes!

Here, a Fast Buying Guide . . .

- **Chicken & turkey** Buy chicken and turkey in small portions, already cooked and ready for eating. Look for such "finds" as packaged teriyaki chicken fillets, Buffalo chicken wings, honey-battered chicken tenders, hand-sliced smoked turkey (a treat and usually always available).

- **Pre-seasoned meat, all ready to cook** Many butchers these days are seasoning up fresh uncooked meats. All you need to do is cook them up in a flash — in the skillet or on the grill. Try blackened steaks, herb-coated marinated chicken breasts and even stuffed pork chops.

- **Salad bar solutions** Look around the salad bar for peeled garlic cloves, ready for mincing; stir-fry vegetable combos, such as snow peas, bell pepper strips and sliced mushrooms, ready for the wok; carrot sticks, ready for blanching and tossing into an orange-honey-butter sauce; chopped onions and peppers, ready for tossing into soups, chilies and stews.

- **Seafood** Look for fresh shrimp that's shelled and deveined. Buy cooked or uncooked, whichever works best with your recipe. Select fillets of fresh fish, such as sole, salmon or tuna. These have been skinned and boned and are ready to cook. Many come already seasoned as well.

- **Anything on a stick** Kabobs . . . they're the fastest answer to homemade dinner! Grab a package of kabobs from the meat or seafood department, then just broil or grill. Depending on the day, you're likely to find all types of "meals on a stick," such as chicken skewered with fresh pineapple, pearl onions and cherry tomatoes; beef sirloin bites with tiny new potatoes, zucchini slices and mushrooms; scallops threaded with snow peas and red bell peppers.

- **Sides** Pick a main dish recipe here, then make a quick stop at a gourmet take-out shop or prepared-food counter to round out supper in a flash. Look for homemade mashed potatoes, stuffed mushrooms, corn pudding, wild rice, fresh vegetable tosses such as zucchini or green beans with cherry tomatoes, grilled veggies, roasted new potatoes, and maybe even fresh-made bread pudding or cherry cobbler for dessert.

5 Ways to Spice up Couscous

Cook up a box of five-minute couscous according to the package's instructions, then toss in a few extra ingredients. Instant meal!

- **Chicken Couscous** Herb chicken-flavored couscous + cooked chicken strips + cooked frozen green peas + grated lemon peel + fresh chopped mint on top.

- **Shrimp & Curry Couscous** Curry-flavored couscous + hot cooked shrimp + dry roasted peanuts. Serve with chutney and plain yogurt.

- **Salad Bar Couscous** Original couscous + steamed broccoli florets + chopped tomatoes + sliced scallions + crumbled feta on top.

- **Couscous Italian** Parmesan-flavored couscous + wedges of salami + strips of roasted red peppers (from the jar) + shredded mozzarella + pesto (from the jar).

- **Mushroom Couscous** Original couscous + sliced mushrooms sautéed in garlic oil + shredded Provolone + chopped fresh thyme (or dried thyme). Choose a mixture of mushrooms, such as: chanterelles, shiitake, and portobellos.

Fish 101

Fish fillets may be the ultimate quick fix — and they're healthy, too. Buy them fresh; they won't need more than a squirt of lemon juice and you're all set.

- **How to cook?** Depends on the texture. Here's a quick breakdown.

  Delicate-to-medium texture — great for baking, pan frying (catfish, flounder, orange roughy, sole, walleye, whitefish).

  Medium firm texture — perfect for broiling, pan-frying, oven-frying (cod, black sea bass, bluefish, Chilean sea bass, haddock/scrod, mahi mahi, perch, red snapper, redfish, rainbow trout, rockfish, salmon, sea bass, shad, tilapia, tilefish).

  Firm texture — best for broiling, grilling (grouper, halibut, monkfish, striped bass, swordfish, tuna).

- **10-minute cooking rule** Cook fish 10 minutes per inch of thickness (measure at thickest point before stuffing or rolling). If using unthawed frozen fish, cook 20 minutes per inch.

- **Cooking in sauce or foil?** Cook 5 minutes more.

- **Is it done yet?** Insert a fork in the thickest part of the fish and gently twist the fork. When the fish flakes, it's done.

Pasta Pronto!

For supper in a flash, you can't beat pasta. Grab it fresh from the refrigerated case at your grocer's or gourmet shop, or use one of the dried pasta varieties suggested below. Cook fresh pasta for just a few minutes, as the package suggests. Then toss with one of these combos until the cheese begins to melt.

- **Spring Pasta** Hot cooked bow-tie pasta + bite-size pieces of fresh steamed asparagus and thin carrot rounds + bites of Brie + freshly snipped parsley

- **Pesto Pot** Hot cooked linguine + thinly sliced plum tomatoes + slivers of salami + pesto (fresh or jarred) + chopped red onion + shredded fresh Romano cheese

- **Pasta Carbonara** Hot cooked spaghetti + lots of crisp crumbled bacon + frozen green peas, heated and drained + sautéed minced garlic + enough heavy cream to make it saucy + shreds of fresh Parmesan cheese

- **Three-Peppered Penne** Hot cooked penne pasta + slivers of green, red and yellow bell peppers blanched in boiling water until crisp-tender + marinara sauce, heated + chopped ripe olives + shredded Provolone cheese

Pizza Tonight!

Turn your kitchen into a pizzeria. Pick a crust: fast, faster or fastest. Spread on some pizza sauce, toss on a few toppings and cover with cheese. Bake, slice and serve. What could be easier?

Step #1 Begin with pizza crust

- **Fast** — Stir together $1^1/_2$ cups original Bisquick® mix with $^1/_3$ cup very hot water and beat until a dough forms. Press into a 12-inch pizza pan.

- **Faster** — Roll out a can of refrigerated pizza crust on a cookie sheet, (read the label to see how!).

- **Fastest** — Buy a ready-to-top pizza crust (original, thin or whole wheat).

Step #2 Sauce it and top it

- Take a cup of pizza sauce, right out of the jar or can. Spread on the crust, from center all the way out to the edges.

  Top it with whatever you like, such as:

- **Italian Sausage & Cheese** Crumbled, cooked Italian sausage, sliced fresh mozzarella and snipped fresh oregano leaves

- **Margherita** Thinly sliced plum tomatoes, shreds of mozzarella, a sprinkling of fresh Parmesan and slivers of fresh basil

- **Chicken Fajita** Strips of cooked chicken, thin red bell pepper strips, finely chopped red onion, a drizzle of hickory smoked barbecue sauce and Monterey Jack or taco shredded cheese

- **Scampi** Cooked medium shrimp (shelled and deveined), minced garlic, sliced green onions, shreds of Provolone cheese and snipped fresh Italian flat-leaf parsley

- **Lebanese** Drained canned garbanzo beans (chick peas), chopped plum tomatoes, chopped ripe olives and crumbled feta

Step #3 Bake until bubbly

Cook the pizza in a hot oven until hot and bubbly:

- **Fast Bisquick Dough** at 450°F for 12 to 15 minutes

- **Faster Refrigerated Pizza Crust** at 425°F for 10 to 12 minutes

- **Fastest Ready-to-Top Pizza Crust** at 450°F for 8 to 10 minutes

Cut with a pizza cutter or kitchen shears. Serve hot!

Italian New Potato Salad

Broiled Portobello Mushroom Salad

Tuscan Panzanella Salad

Caesar Salad

Bacon-Spinach Salad

Spinach-Mango Salad

Fruity Chicken Salad with Mixed Greens and Pecans

Crunchy Oriental Chicken Salad

Wild Rice–Chicken Salad

Southwestern Chicken BLT Salad

Buffalo Chicken Salad

Caribbean Shrimp Salad

Gyro Salad

Asian Steak Salad

Grilled Steak and Potato Salad

Fajita Salad

1
salad bar

Italian New Potato Salad

Prep Time: 30 min ▪ Start to Finish: 30 min ▪ 8 Servings

³/₄ lb green beans
10 to 12 new potatoes (1¹/₂ lb), cut into fourths
¹/₄ cup water
¹/₂ cup Italian dressing or balsamic vinaigrette
¹/₄ cup chopped red onion
1 can (2¹/₄ oz) sliced ripe olives, drained

1 Cut beans in half if desired. Place beans, potatoes and water in 2-quart microwavable casserole. Cover and microwave on High 10 to 12 minutes, rotating dish ¹/₂ turn every 4 minutes, until potatoes are tender; drain.

2 Place beans and potatoes in large glass or plastic bowl. Pour dressing over vegetables; toss. Add onion and olives; toss.

No mayo on your potato salad? No worries — it's delicious and very cosmopolitan.

1 Serving: Calories 125 (Calories from Fat 65); Total Fat 7g (Saturated Fat 1g); Cholesterol 0mg; Sodium 210mg; Total Carbohydrate 17g (Dietary Fiber 3g); Protein 2g

Broiled Portobello Mushroom Salad

Prep Time: 20 min ▪ Start to Finish: 20 min ▪ 4 Servings

$^1/_2$ cup Italian dressing
$^3/_4$ lb sliced fresh portabella mushrooms
4 cups bite-size pieces mixed salad greens
$^1/_2$ cup crumbled herbed or plain chèvre (goat) cheese (2 oz)
$^1/_2$ cup shredded mozzarella cheese (2 oz)
4 slices French bread, toasted and cut in half
4 plum (Roma) tomatoes, sliced

1 Set oven control to broil. Spray broiler pan rack with cooking spray. Brush dressing on both sides of mushrooms; reserve remaining dressing. Place mushrooms on rack in broiler pan. Broil with tops 2 to 4 inches from heat 4 minutes; turn. Broil about 3 minutes longer or just until mushrooms are tender.

2 Meanwhile, divide salad greens among 4 plates. In small bowl, mix cheeses; spread on toast.

3 Place mushrooms on salad greens. Top with tomatoes. Drizzle with remaining dressing. Serve with toast.

1 Serving: Calories 430 (Calories from Fat 190); Total Fat 21g (Saturated Fat 5g); Cholesterol 25mg; Sodium 890mg; Total Carbohydrate 43g (Dietary Fiber 5g); Protein 16g

Tuscan Panzanella Salad

Prep Time: 15 min ▪ Start to Finish: 15 min ▪ 6 Servings

1 bag (10 oz) romaine and leaf lettuce mix
1 can (19 oz) cannellini beans, rinsed and drained
2 cups large croutons
1 cup sweet grape tomatoes
$\frac{1}{2}$ cup thinly sliced red onion
$\frac{1}{3}$ cup pitted kalamata olives, cut in half
$\frac{1}{3}$ cup balsamic vinaigrette

1 Mix all ingredients except vinaigrette in large bowl.

2 Add vinaigrette; toss until coated.

1 Serving: Calories 250 (Calories from Fat 80); Total Fat 9g (Saturated Fat 1g); Cholesterol 5mg; Sodium 360mg; Total Carbohydrate 36g (Dietary Fiber 8g); Protein 12g

Caesar Salad

Prep Time: 15 min ▪ Start to Finish: 15 min ▪ 6 Servings

1 clove garlic, cut in half
8 anchovy fillets, cut up, or 2 teaspoons anchovy paste
$1/3$ cup olive or vegetable oil
3 tablespoons lemon juice
1 teaspoon Worcestershire sauce
$1/4$ teaspoon salt
$1/4$ teaspoon ground mustard
Freshly ground pepper
1 large or 2 small bunches romaine lettuce, torn into bite-size pieces (10 cups)
1 cup garlic-flavored croutons
$1/3$ cup grated Parmesan cheese

1 Rub large wooden salad bowl with cut clove of garlic. Allow a few small pieces of garlic to remain in bowl if desired.

2 In salad bowl, mix anchovies, oil, lemon juice, Worcestershire sauce, salt, mustard and pepper.

3 Add romaine; toss until coated. Sprinkle with croutons and cheese; toss.

Look — no raw egg! The salad still has all the great taste, without any of the safety issues.

1 Serving: Calories 190 (Calories from Fat 140); Total Fat 16g (Saturated Fat 3g); Cholesterol 10mg; Sodium 500mg; Total Carbohydrate 7g (Dietary Fiber 2g); Protein 6g

Bacon-Spinach Salad

Prep Time: 25 min ▪ Start to Finish: 25 min ▪ 6 Servings

4 slices bacon, cut into $1/2$-inch pieces
3 tablespoons vegetable oil
5 medium green onions, chopped ($1/3$ cup)
2 teaspoons sugar
$1/2$ teaspoon salt
$1/4$ teaspoon pepper
2 tablespoons white or cider vinegar
8 oz washed fresh spinach leaves (9 cups)
2 hard-cooked eggs, sliced

1 In 10-inch skillet, cook bacon over medium heat, stirring occasionally, until crisp. Remove bacon with slotted spoon; drain on paper towels. Drain all but 3 tablespoons bacon fat from skillet (if there isn't 3 tablespoons bacon fat remaining, add enough vegetable oil to bacon fat to equal 3 tablespoons).

2 Add oil, onions, sugar, salt and pepper to bacon fat in skillet. Cook over medium heat 2 to 3 minutes, stirring occasionally, until onions are slightly softened. Stir in vinegar.

3 Place spinach in very large bowl. Pour warm dressing over spinach; toss to coat. Arrange egg slices on top; sprinkle with bacon.

Buy bags of pre-washed spinach and skip the cleaning step.

1 Serving: Calories 140 (Calories from Fat 100); Total Fat 11g (Saturated Fat 2.5g); Cholesterol 75mg; Sodium 150mg; Total Carbohydrate 4g (Dietary Fiber 2g); Protein 5g

Spinach-Mango Salad

Prep Time: 10 min ▪ Start to Finish: 10 min ▪ 6 Servings

1 tablespoon canola or soybean oil

2 tablespoons cider vinegar

$1/3$ cup peach or apricot preserves

$1/2$ teaspoon salt

1 bag (6 oz) baby spinach leaves

2 mangoes, cut lengthwise in half, seed removed and cut up (2 cups)

$1/2$ cup very thinly sliced red onion

$1/2$ cup golden raisins

1 In small bowl, beat oil, vinegar, preserves and salt with wire whisk or fork until blended.

2 In large bowl, toss remaining ingredients. Pour dressing over spinach mixture, tossing gently to coat.

1 Serving: Calories 170 (Calories from Fat 25); Total Fat 2.5g (Saturated Fat 0g); Cholesterol 0mg; Sodium 230mg; Total Carbohydrate 36g (Dietary Fiber 3g); Protein 2g

Fruity Chicken Salad with Mixed Greens and Pecans

Prep Time: 20 min   Start to Finish: 20 min   4 Servings

2 boneless skinless chicken breasts (4 oz each)
1 cup cut-up red grapes
2 medium stalks celery, thinly sliced (1 cup)
1/2 cup dried cherries or cranberries
1/4 cup finely chopped onion
3/4 cup fat-free honey-mustard dressing or other fat-free dressing
8 cups mixed greens
1/4 cup chopped pecans, toasted*

1 Heat gas or charcoal grill. Place chicken on grill. Cover grill; cook over medium heat 7 to 10 minutes, turning halfway through cooking, until juice of chicken is clear when center of thickest part is cut. Cool; cut into bite-size pieces.

2 In large bowl, mix chicken, grapes, celery, cherries, onion and 1/2 cup of the dressing.

3 Divide greens among 4 plates. Top with chicken mixture; sprinkle with pecans. Drizzle each salad with 1 tablespoon dressing.

*To toast nuts, spread in ungreased shallow pan and bake at 350°F for 5 to 10 minutes, stirring occasionally, until nuts are light brown and aromatic.

Don't want to fire up the grill? Just use any cooked chicken — you'll need about 1 cup.

1 Serving: Calories 300 (Calories from Fat 70); Total Fat 7g (Saturated Fat 1g); Cholesterol 35mg; Sodium 600mg; Total Carbohydrate 42g (Dietary Fiber 6g); Protein 16g

Crunchy Oriental Chicken Salad

Prep Time: 15 min ▮ Start to Finish: 15 min ▮ 6 Servings

2 tablespoons butter or margarine

1 package (3 oz) Oriental-flavor ramen noodle soup mix

2 tablespoons sesame seed

$1/4$ cup sugar

$1/4$ cup white vinegar

1 tablespoon sesame or vegetable oil

$1/2$ teaspoon pepper

2 cups cut-up cooked chicken

$1/4$ cup dry-roasted peanuts, if desired

4 medium green onions, sliced ($1/4$ cup)

1 bag (16 oz) coleslaw mix

1 can (11 oz) mandarin orange segments, drained

1 In 10-inch skillet, melt butter over medium heat. Stir in seasoning packet from soup mix. Break block of noodles into bite-size pieces over skillet; stir into butter mixture.

2 Cook noodles 2 minutes, stirring occasionally. Stir in sesame seed. Cook about 2 minutes longer, stirring occasionally, until noodles are golden brown; remove from heat.

3 In large glass or plastic bowl, mix sugar, vinegar, oil and pepper. Add noodle mixture and remaining ingredients; toss.

1 Serving: Calories 290 (Calories from Fat 120); Total Fat 13g (Saturated Fat 4g); Cholesterol 50mg; Sodium 260mg; Total Carbohydrate 26g (Dietary Fiber 3g); Protein 16g

Wild Rice–Chicken Salad

Prep Time: 15 min ▪ Start to Finish: 15 min ▪ 4 Servings

Basil Vinaigrette

$1/4$ cup olive or vegetable oil

3 tablespoons raspberry vinegar or red wine vinegar

1 tablespoon chopped fresh basil leaves

$1/4$ teaspoon salt

$1/4$ teaspoon pepper

Salad

1 pint (2 cups) deli chicken salad

1 can (15 oz) cooked wild rice, drained

$1/2$ cup dried cranberries

Boston lettuce leaves

1 Make vinaigrette by mixing all of the ingredients in small bowl.

2 Mix remaining ingredients except lettuce in large bowl. Toss with vinaigrette until coated. Serve on lettuce.

1 Serving: Calories 475 (Calories from Fat 235); Total Fat 26g (Saturated Fat 4g); Cholesterol 45mg; Sodium 380mg; Total Carbohydrate 42g (Dietary Fiber 4g); Protein 18g

Go ahead and save time: use cooked wild rice in cans instead of cooking regular wild rice. A 15-ounce can contains about 2 cups of wild rice.

Southwestern Chicken BLT Salad

Prep Time: 20 min ▪ Start to Finish: 20 min ▪ 6 Servings

Salsa-Bacon Dressing

1/2 cup chunky-style salsa

1/2 cup nonfat ranch dressing

1 tablespoon chopped fresh parsley

Salad

1 bag (10 oz) romaine and leaf lettuce mix

2 packages (6 oz each) refrigerated cooked Southwest-flavor chicken breast
strips

4 plum (Roma) tomatoes, coarsely chopped

1/2 cup chopped cooked bacon

1/2 cup croutons

1 Make dressing by mixing ingredients in small bowl; set aside.

2 Mix remaining ingredients in large bowl. Add dressing; toss until coated.

1 Serving: Calories 190 (Calories from Fat 60); Total Fat 7g (Saturated Fat 2g); Cholesterol 55mg;
Sodium 530mg; Total Carbohydrate 12g (Dietary Fiber 2g); Protein 21g

Save some chopping time — use 1 cup cherry tomatoes, cut in half, instead of the roma tomatoes.

Buffalo Chicken Salad

Prep Time: 15 min ▪ Start to Finish: 15 min ▪ 4 Servings

1 package (9 oz) frozen breaded chicken breast tenders
1 tablespoon chili powder
2 cups shredded lettuce
2 cups carrot sticks
2 cups celery sticks
2 cups broccoli florets
2 cups sliced cucumbers (2 small)
1 bottle (8 oz) blue cheese dressing (1 cup)

1 Place chicken and chili powder in resealable plastic food-storage bag; seal bag and shake well to coat. Prepare chicken as directed on package.

2 Arrange lettuce on large serving platter. Top with vegetables and cooked chicken. Serve with dressing.

1 Serving: Calories 540 (Calories from Fat 360); Total Fat 40g (Saturated Fat 5g); Cholesterol 50mg; Sodium 1140mg; Total Carbohydrate 30g (Dietary Fiber 6g); Protein 15g

Caribbean Shrimp Salad

Prep Time: 20 min ▪ Start to Finish: 20 min ▪ 4 Servings

Honey Lime Dressing

3 tablespoons honey

1 teaspoon grated lime peel

2 tablespoons lime juice

1 tablespoon vegetable oil

1 to 2 teaspoons finely chopped jalapeño chile

1/4 teaspoon salt

Salad

1 bag (5 oz) mixed greens

1 lb cooked peeled deveined medium shrimp, thawed if frozen and
tails removed

1 small red onion, thinly sliced

1 can (15 1/4 oz) pineapple shapes, drained

1 cup snow pea pods

1 Make dressing by mixing all ingredients.

2 Mix remaining ingredients in large bowl. Add dressing; toss until coated.

Don't have pineapple shapes? You can substitute
pineapple tidbits and it works just as well.

1 Serving: Calories 285 (Calories from Fat 45); Total Fat 5 (Saturated Fat 1g); Cholesterol 220mg;
Sodium 410mg; Total Carbohydrate 34g (Dietary Fiber 2g); Protein 26g

Gyro Salad

Prep Time: 25 min ▪ Start to Finish: 25 min ▪ 6 Servings

Yogurt Dressing
$1/2$ cup plain fat-free yogurt
$1/2$ cup reduced-fat sour cream
$1/4$ cup fat-free (skim) milk
1 teaspoon Greek seasoning

Salad
1-lb beef boneless sirloin steak, 1 to $1^1/2$ inches thick
1 tablespoon canola or soybean oil
$1^1/4$ teaspoons Greek seasoning
8 cups torn mixed salad greens
1 medium cucumber, thinly sliced ($1^1/2$ cups)
1 small red onion, thinly sliced and separated into rings
1 large tomato, chopped (1 cup)

1 Make dressing by mixing all ingredients in small bowl with wire whisk until creamy; set aside.

2 Cut beef across grain into 4×$1/4$-inch strips. Heat oil in 12-inch nonstick skillet over medium-high heat. Add beef to skillet; sprinkle with Greek seasoning. Cook, about 5 minutes, stirring frequently, until beef is brown. Drain if necessary.

3 Arrange salad greens on serving platter or individual serving plates. Top with cucumber, onion, tomato and beef. Serve with dressing.

1 Serving: Calories 180 (Calories from Fat 70); Total Fat 7g (Saturated Fat 2.5g); Cholesterol 50mg; Sodium 80mg; Total Carbohydrate 9g (Dietary Fiber 3g); Protein 19g

Asian Steak Salad

Prep Time: 30 min   Start to Finish: 30 min   6 Servings

1 lb cut-up beef for stir-fry
1 package (3 oz) Oriental-flavor ramen noodle soup mix
$^1/_2$ cup Asian marinade and dressing
1 bag (10 oz) romaine and leaf lettuce mix
1 cup snow pea pods
$^1/_2$ cup matchstick-cut carrots (from 10-oz bag)
1 can (11 oz) mandarin orange segments, drained

1 Spray 12-inch nonstick skillet with cooking spray; heat over medium-high heat. Place beef in skillet; sprinkle with 1 teaspoon seasoning mix from soup mix. (Discard remaining seasoning mix.) Cook beef 4 to 6 minutes, stirring occasionally, until brown. Stir in 1 tablespoon of the dressing.

2 Break block of noodles into small pieces. Mix lettuce, pea pods, carrots, orange segments and uncooked noodles from soup mix. Add remaining dressing; toss until well coated. Divide mixture among 6 plates; top with beef strips.

If you can't find the beef for stir-fry, cut 1 pound beef boneless sirloin into thin strips.

1 Serving: Calories 240 (Calories from Fat 90); Total Fat 10g (Saturated Fat 2g); Cholesterol 40mg; Sodium 360mg; Total Carbohydrate 20g (Dietary Fiber 3g); Protein 18g

Grilled Steak and Potato Salad

Prep Time: 30 min ▪ Start to Finish: 30 min ▪ 4 Servings

3/4 lb small red potatoes, cut in half

2/3 cup honey Dijon dressing

1 boneless beef top sirloin or round steak, 3/4 inch thick (3/4 lb)

1/4 teaspoon salt

1/4 teaspoon coarsely ground pepper

4 cups bite-size pieces romaine lettuce

2 medium tomatoes, cut into thin wedges

1/2 cup thinly sliced red onion

1 Heat gas or charcoal grill. In 2- or 2½-quart saucepan, place potatoes; add enough water to cover potatoes. Heat to boiling; reduce heat to medium. Cook uncovered 5 to 8 minutes or just until potatoes are tender.

2 Drain potatoes; place in medium bowl. Add 2 tablespoons of the dressing; toss to coat. Place potatoes in grill basket (grill "wok") if desired. Brush beef steak with 1 tablespoon of the dressing; sprinkle with salt and pepper.

3 Place beef and potatoes on grill. Cover grill; cook over medium heat 8 to 15 minutes, turning once, until beef is desired doneness and potatoes are golden brown. Cut beef into thin slices.

4 Among 4 plates, divide lettuce, tomatoes and onion. Top with beef and potatoes; drizzle with remaining dressing. Sprinkle with additional pepper if desired.

Try adding a generous sprinkle of crumbled blue or Gorgonzola cheese to top these salads.

1 Serving: Calories 360 (Calories from Fat 180); Total Fat 20g (Saturated Fat 4g); Cholesterol 35mg; Sodium 440mg; Total Carbohydrate 25g (Dietary Fiber 4g); Protein 22g

Fajita Salad

Prep Time: 20 min ■ Start to Finish: 20 min ■ 4 Servings

³/₄ lb lean beef boneless sirloin steak

1 tablespoon vegetable oil

2 medium bell peppers, cut into strips

1 small onion, thinly sliced

4 cups bite-size pieces salad greens

¹/₃ cup Italian dressing

¹/₄ cup plain yogurt

1 Cut beef with grain into 2-inch strips; cut strips across grain into ¹/₈-inch slices.

2 Heat oil in 10-inch nonstick skillet over medium-high heat. Cook beef in oil about 3 minutes, stirring occasionally, until brown. Remove beef from skillet.

3 Cook bell peppers and onion in same skillet about 3 minutes, stirring occasionally, until bell peppers are crisp-tender. Stir in beef.

4 Place salad greens on serving platter. Top with beef mixture. Mix dressing and yogurt; drizzle over salad.

Check out the meat case for precut meats. In addition to being a time-saver, these precut meats often come in small, one-time-use portions, which increases your options.

1 Serving: Calories 255 (Calories from Fat 135); Total Fat 15g (Saturated Fat 2g); Cholesterol 50mg; Sodium 240mg; Total Carbohydrate 10g (Dietary Fiber 3g); Protein 20g

2

great grains
and pasta

Polenta with Italian Vegetables

Prep Time: 30 min ▪ Start to Finish: 30 min ▪ 6 Servings

1 cup yellow cornmeal
³/₄ cup cold water
2¹/₂ cups boiling water
¹/₂ teaspoon salt
²/₃ cup shredded Swiss cheese
2 teaspoons olive or vegetable oil
2 medium zucchini or yellow summer squash, sliced (4 cups)
1 medium red bell pepper, chopped (1 cup)
1 small onion, chopped (¹/₄ cup)
1 clove garlic, finely chopped
¹/₄ cup chopped fresh or 1 tablespoon dried basil leaves
1 can (about 14 oz) artichoke hearts, drained

1 Beat cornmeal and cold water in 2-quart saucepan with wire whisk. Stir in boiling water and salt. Cook over medium-high heat, stirring constantly, until mixture thickens and boils; reduce heat. Cover and simmer 10 minutes, stirring occasionally. Stir in cheese until smooth; keep polenta warm.

2 Heat oil in 10-inch nonstick skillet over medium-high heat. Cook zucchini, bell pepper, onion and garlic in oil about 5 minutes, stirring occasionally, until vegetables are crisp-tender. Stir in basil and artichoke hearts. Serve vegetable mixture over polenta.

1 Serving: Calories 175 (Calories from Fat 45); Total Fat 5g (Saturated Fat 2g); Cholesterol 10mg; Sodium 430mg; Total Carbohydrate 30g (Dietary Fiber 7g); Protein 9g

Onion and Mushroom Quinoa

Prep Time: 30 min ▪ Start to Finish: 30 min ▪ 4 Servings

1 teaspoon canola or soybean oil
1 cup uncooked quinoa, rinsed
1 small onion, cut into fourths and sliced
1 medium carrot, shredded ($^2/_3$ cup)
1 small green bell pepper, chopped ($^1/_2$ cup)
1 cup sliced fresh mushrooms (about 2$^1/_2$ oz)
1 teaspoon chopped fresh or $^1/_4$ teaspoon dried thyme leaves
$^1/_4$ teaspoon salt
1 can (14 oz) fat-free vegetable broth

1 Heat oil in 2-quart saucepan over medium heat. Cook quinoa and onion in oil 4 to 5 minutes, stirring occasionally, until light brown.

2 Stir in remaining ingredients. Heat to boiling; reduce heat to low. Cover and simmer about 15 minutes or until liquid is absorbed. Fluff with fork.

It's worth taking time to rinse the quinoa, as it has a bitter coating that comes right off in water.

1 Serving: Calories 200 (Calories from Fat 35); Total Fat 4g (Saturated Fat 0g); Cholesterol 0mg; Sodium 600mg; Total Carbohydrate 35g (Dietary Fiber 4g); Protein 7g

Mediterranean Couscous and Beans

Prep Time: 10 min ▪ Start to Finish: 15 min ▪ 4 Servings

3 cups vegetable or chicken broth
2 cups uncooked couscous
$1/2$ cup raisins or currants
$1/4$ teaspoon pepper
$1/8$ teaspoon ground red pepper (cayenne)
1 small tomato, chopped ($1/2$ cup)
1 can (15 oz) chick peas, rinsed and drained
$1/3$ cup crumbled feta cheese

1 In 3-quart saucepan, heat broth to boiling. Stir in remaining ingredients except cheese; remove from heat.

2 Cover and let stand about 5 minutes or until liquid is absorbed; stir gently.

3 Sprinkle each serving with cheese.

1 Serving: Calories 600 (Calories from Fat 60); Total Fat 6g (Saturated Fat 2.5g); Cholesterol 10mg; Sodium 1050mg; Total Carbohydrate 114g (Dietary Fiber 12g); Protein 23g

Kasha and Beef Supper

Prep Time: 25 min   Start to Finish: 25 min   4 Servings

2 cups beef broth

1 cup uncooked kasha (roasted buckwheat groats)

$1/2$ lb extra-lean (at least 90%) ground beef

1 medium stalk celery, sliced ($1/2$ cup)

4 medium green onions, sliced ($1/4$ cup)

1 can ($14 1/2$ oz) diced tomatoes with crushed red pepper and basil, undrained

$1/4$ teaspoon pepper

1 Heat broth to boiling in 2-quart saucepan. Stir in kasha; reduce heat to medium. Cover and cook about 7 minutes or until tender; drain if needed.

2 Meanwhile, cook beef, celery and green onions in 10-inch nonstick skillet over medium heat 8 to 10 minutes, stirring frequently, until beef is thoroughly cooked; drain.

3 Stir tomatoes and pepper into beef mixture. Heat to boiling; reduce heat. Cover and simmer 5 minutes. Stir in kasha; cook until thoroughly heated.

1 Serving: Calories 230 (Calories from Fat 50); Total Fat 6g (Saturated Fat 2g); Cholesterol 35mg; Sodium 840mg; Total Carbohydrate 29g (Dietary Fiber 4g); Protein 17g

Pork Fried Rice

Prep Time: 25 min ▪ Start to Finish: 25 min ▪ 4 Servings

1 cup bean sprouts
2 tablespoons vegetable oil
1 cup sliced fresh mushrooms (3 oz)
3 cups cold cooked regular long-grain rice
1 cup cut-up cooked pork
2 medium green onions, sliced (2 tablespoons)
2 large eggs, slightly beaten
3 tablespoons soy sauce
Dash of white pepper

1 Rinse bean sprouts with cold water; drain.

2 In 10-inch skillet, heat 1 tablespoon of the oil over medium heat; rotate skillet until oil covers bottom. Cook mushrooms in oil about 1 minute, stirring frequently, until coated.

3 Add bean sprouts, rice, pork and onions to skillet. Cook over medium heat about 5 minutes, stirring and breaking up rice, until hot.

4 Move rice mixture to side of skillet. Add remaining 1 tablespoon oil to other side of skillet. Cook eggs in oil over medium heat, stirring constantly, until eggs are thickened throughout but still moist. Stir eggs into rice mixture. Stir in soy sauce and pepper.

This dish is perfect for leftover rice — think takeout leftovers — as cold rice allows the grains to stay separate during frying and keeps the rice from getting mushy.

1 Serving: Calories 360 (Calories from Fat 130); Total Fat 14g (Saturated Fat 3.5g); Cholesterol 135mg; Sodium 1190mg; Total Carbohydrate 37g (Dietary Fiber 1g); Protein 20g

Wild Rice–Pecan Patties

Prep Time: 20 min ▪ Start to Finish: 20 min ▪ 4 Servings (2 patties each)

2 cups cooked wild rice

1 cup soft bread crumbs (about 1$^1/_2$ slices bread)

$^1/_3$ cup chopped pecans

$^1/_2$ teaspoon garlic salt

2 eggs

1 jar (2$^1/_2$ oz) mushroom pieces and stems, drained and finely chopped

1 jar (2 oz) diced pimientos, drained

2 tablespoons vegetable oil

1 Mix all ingredients except oil.

2 Heat oil in 10-inch skillet over medium heat. Scoop wild rice mixture by $^1/_3$ cupfuls into skillet; flatten to $^1/_2$ inch. Cook about 3 minutes on each side or until light brown. Remove patties from skillet; cover and keep warm while cooking remaining patties.

Try serving these different patties in sandwich buns topped with cranberry sauce.

2 Patties: Calories 340 (Calories from Fat 150); Total Fat 17g (Saturated Fat 2g); Cholesterol 105mg; Sodium 450mg; Total Carbohydrate 41g (Dietary Fiber 4g); Protein 11g

Chili Beef 'n' Pasta

Prep Time: 20 min   Start to Finish: 20 min   4 Servings

2¹/₂ cups uncooked rotini pasta (8 oz)
1 lb lean (at least 80%) ground beef
1 medium onion, chopped (¹/₂ cup)
1 can (11.25 oz) condensed fiesta chili beef with beans soup
1 jar (8 oz) salsa (1 cup)
¹/₂ cup water
1 cup shredded Cheddar cheese (4 oz)

1 Cook and drain pasta as directed on package.

2 Meanwhile, in 12-inch skillet, cook beef and onion over medium-high heat, stirring occasionally, until beef is brown; drain. Reduce heat to medium. Stir soup, salsa and water into beef. Cook until thoroughly heated.

3 Serve beef mixture over pasta. Sprinkle with cheese.

1 Serving: Calories 660 (Calories from Fat 240); Total Fat 26g (Saturated Fat 12g); Cholesterol 110mg; Sodium 1260mg; Total Carbohydrate 65g (Dietary Fiber 6g); Protein 40g

Ravioli and Vegetables with Pesto Cream

Prep Time: 20 min ▌ Start to Finish: 20 min ▌ 4 Servings

2 teaspoons olive or vegetable oil

8 oz green beans, cut into 1½-inch pieces

½ medium yellow bell pepper, cut into ½-inch pieces (½ cup)

3 plum (Roma) tomatoes, cut into ½-inch pieces (1 cup)

½ teaspoon salt

16 oz frozen cheese-filled ravioli (from 25 to 27½ oz bag)

½ cup sour cream

3 tablespoons basil pesto

2 teaspoons grated lemon peel

1 In 12-inch nonstick skillet, heat oil over medium-high heat. Cook green beans and bell pepper in oil about 5 minutes, stirring frequently, until crisp-tender. Stir in tomatoes and salt. Cook 3 minutes.

2 Meanwhile, cook ravioli as directed on package. In small bowl, mix sour cream, basil pesto and lemon peel.

3 Drain ravioli; return to saucepan. Toss ravioli, vegetable mixture and sour cream mixture.

1 Serving: Calories 380 (Calories from Fat 210); Total Fat 24g (Saturated Fat 9g); Cholesterol 135mg; Sodium 1350mg; Total Carbohydrate 26g (Dietary Fiber 3g); Protein 16g

Great Grains and Pasta

Fettuccine with Ricotta, Tomato and Basil

Prep Time: 15 min   Start to Finish: 15 min   6 Servings

2 packages (9 oz each) refrigerated fettuccine
6 tablespoons butter or margarine, melted
1^1/$_2$ cups ricotta cheese
1 cup grated Parmesan cheese
2 large tomatoes, seeded and chopped (2 cups)
^{1}/$_4$ cup coarsely chopped fresh basil leaves

1 Cook and drain fettuccine as directed on package, using 4-quart saucepan. Return to saucepan.

2 In small bowl, mix butter, ricotta cheese and ^{3}/$_4$ cup of the Parmesan cheese; toss with fettuccine.

3 Serve fettuccine topped with tomatoes, basil and remaining ^{1}/$_4$ cup Parmesan cheese.

1 Serving: Calories 570 (Calories from Fat 220); Total Fat 25g (Saturated Fat 13g); Cholesterol 135mg; Sodium 480mg; Total Carbohydrate 62g (Dietary Fiber 3g); Protein 25g

Spaghetti Puttanesca

Prep Time: 10 min ■ Start to Finish: 25 min ■ 4 Servings

$^1/_3$ cup olive or vegetable oil

2 cloves garlic, cut in half

1 tablespoon capers

4 flat fillets of anchovy in oil, drained

2 cans (28 oz each) whole Italian-style tomatoes, drained and chopped

1 small red or green jalapeño chile, seeded and finely chopped

$^1/_2$ cup sliced kalamata or ripe olives

1 package (16 oz) spaghetti

1 Heat oil in Dutch oven over medium-high heat. Cook garlic in oil, stirring frequently, until golden. Remove garlic and discard.

2 Stir capers, anchovy fillets, tomatoes and chile into oil in Dutch oven. Heat to boiling; reduce heat. Simmer uncovered 15 minutes. Stir in olives; keep warm.

3 While sauce is simmering, cook and drain spaghetti as directed on package. Stir spaghetti into tomato mixture; cook until hot.

1 Serving: Calories 735 (Calories from Fat 205); Total Fat 23g (Saturated Fat 4g); Cholesterol 5mg; Sodium 1410mg; Total Carbohydrate 120g (Dietary Fiber 8g); Protein 20g

Kung Pao Pork over Sesame Noodles

Prep Time: 30 min ▪ Start to Finish: 30 min ▪ 4 Servings

1 tablespoon vegetable oil
1 bag (16 oz) broccoli slaw mix or 1 bag (16 oz) coleslaw mix
1 lb pork boneless loin, cut into $^{1}/_{2}$-inch pieces
1 medium red bell pepper, cut into $^{1}/_{2}$-inch pieces
$^{1}/_{2}$ cup water
$^{1}/_{2}$ cup spicy Szechuan stir-fry sauce
1 tablespoon honey
1 package (6 or 7 oz) rice stick noodles
2 teaspoons sesame or vegetable oil
2 tablespoons salted peanuts

1 Heat 12-inch nonstick skillet over medium-high heat. Add vegetable oil; rotate skillet to coat bottom. Add broccoli slaw; stir-fry 2 to 3 minutes or until crisp-tender. Remove broccoli slaw from skillet; keep warm.

2 Add pork to same skillet; stir-fry over medium-high heat 5 to 6 minutes or until brown. Stir in bell pepper and water. Cover and cook 3 to 4 minutes, stirring occasionally, until pork is tender. Stir in stir-fry sauce and honey; reduce heat. Simmer uncovered 1 to 2 minutes.

3 Meanwhile, in 4-quart Dutch oven, heat 3 quarts water to boiling. Add noodles. Boil 3 minutes; drain. In large bowl, toss noodles and sesame oil. Divide noodles among 4 individual serving bowls. Top with broccoli slaw and pork mixture. Sprinkle with peanuts.

Rice stick noodles are fast cookers — they can save you precious minutes on a busy day.

1 Serving: Calories 510 (Calories from Fat 160); Total Fat 18g (Saturated Fat 4.5g); Cholesterol 70mg; Sodium 1480mg; Total Carbohydrate 55g (Dietary Fiber 6g); Protein 33g

Rice Noodles with Peanut Sauce

Prep Time: 16 min ▪ Start to Finish: 16 min ▪ 4 Servings

8 oz rice stick noodles
$1/2$ cup creamy peanut butter
2 tablespoons soy sauce
1 teaspoon grated gingerroot
$1/2$ teaspoon crushed red pepper
$1/2$ cup vegetable or chicken broth
1 cup shredded carrots ($1^1/2$ medium)
1 small red bell pepper, cut into $1/4$-inch strips
2 medium green onions, sliced (2 tablespoons)
2 tablespoons chopped fresh cilantro, if desired

1 In 3-quart saucepan, heat 2 quarts water to boiling. Break noodles in half and pull apart slightly; drop into boiling water. Cook uncovered 1 minute; drain. Rinse with cold water; drain.

2 In small bowl, beat peanut butter, soy sauce, gingerroot and crushed red pepper with wire whisk until smooth. Gradually beat in broth.

3 Place noodles in large bowl. Add peanut butter mixture, carrots, bell pepper and onions; toss. Sprinkle with cilantro.

You'll love this new use for your faithful jar of peanut butter.

1 Serving: Calories 470 (Calories from Fat 170); Total Fat 19g (Saturated Fat 3.5g); Cholesterol 0mg; Sodium 770mg; Total Carbohydrate 60g (Dietary Fiber 5g); Protein 14g

Asian Noodle Bowl

Prep Time: 30 min ▪ Start to Finish: 30 min ▪ 4 Servings

$^{1}/_{4}$ cup barbecue sauce

2 tablespoons hoisin sauce

1 tablespoon peanut butter

Dash of ground red pepper
     (cayenne), if desired

1 tablespoon vegetable oil

1 small onion, cut into thin wedges

$^{1}/_{4}$ cup chopped red bell pepper

2 cups broccoli florets

$^{3}/_{4}$ cup water

$^{1}/_{2}$ teaspoon salt, if desired

1 package (10 oz) Chinese curly noodles

1 can (14 oz) baby corn cobs, drained

$^{1}/_{4}$ cup chopped peanuts

1 In medium bowl, mix barbecue sauce, hoisin sauce, peanut butter and ground red pepper; set aside.

2 In 12-inch skillet, heat oil over medium heat 1 to 2 minutes. Cook onion and bell pepper in oil 2 minutes, stirring frequently. Stir in broccoli and $^{3}/_{4}$ cup water. Cover and cook 4 to 6 minutes, stirring occasionally, until broccoli is crisp-tender.

3 Meanwhile, fill 4-quart Dutch oven about half full with water; add salt. Cover and heat to boiling over high heat. Add noodles; heat to boiling. Boil uncovered 4 to 5 minutes, stirring frequently, until noodles are tender.

4 While noodles are cooking, stir corn and sauce mixture into vegetable mixture. Cook uncovered 3 to 4 minutes, stirring occasionally, until mixture is hot and bubbly.

5 Drain noodles. Divide noodles among 4 individual serving bowls. Spoon vegetable mixture over noodles. Sprinkle with peanuts.

1 Serving: Calories 520 (Calories from Fat 130); Total Fat 14g (Saturated Fat 2.5g); Cholesterol 60mg; Sodium 980mg; Total Carbohydrate 80g (Dietary Fiber 7g); Protein 17g

Spinach and Chicken Skillet

Chicken Piccata

Italian White Beans with Chicken

Southwestern Chicken Scaloppine

Caesar Chicken with Orzo

Lemon Chicken with Olives

Spicy Chicken with Broccoli

Greek Turkey Burgers with Yogurt Sauce

Italian Steak Sandwiches

Onion-Topped Caesar Burgers

Mini Meat Loaves

Filet of Beef with Mustard-Herb Crust

Orange Teriyaki Beef with Noodles

Spanish Lamb and Couscous

Breaded Pork Chops

Pork Chops with Green Chile Corn

Pork and White Bean Cassoulet

Cajun Pork Burgers

Pork Lo Mein

3

easy chicken and meat

Spinach and Chicken Skillet

Prep Time: 30 min ▪ Start to Finish: 30 min ▪ 6 Servings

6 boneless skinless chicken breasts (about 1³/₄ lb)
1 cup fat-free (skim) milk
¹/₂ cup fat-free chicken broth
1 medium onion, chopped (¹/₂ cup)
1 bag (10 oz) washed fresh spinach, chopped
¹/₄ teaspoon salt
¹/₄ teaspoon pepper
¹/₄ teaspoon ground nutmeg

1 Heat 12-inch nonstick skillet over medium heat. Cook chicken in skillet 2 minutes on each side; reduce heat to medium-low. Stir in milk, broth and onion. Cook about 5 minutes, turning chicken occasionally, until onion is tender.

2 Stir in spinach. Cook 3 to 4 minutes, stirring occasionally, until spinach is completely wilted and juice of chicken is clear when center of thickest part is cut. Remove chicken from skillet; keep warm.

3 Increase heat to medium. Cook spinach mixture about 3 minutes or until liquid has almost evaporated. Stir in salt, pepper and nutmeg. Serve chicken on spinach. Sprinkle with additional pepper if desired.

1 Serving: Calories 190 (Calories from Fat 40); Total Fat 4.5g (Saturated Fat 1.5g); Cholesterol 80mg; Sodium 260mg; Total Carbohydrate 5g (Dietary Fiber 1g); Protein 32g

Chicken Piccata

Prep Time: 25 min ■ Start to Finish: 25 min ■ 4 Servings

4 boneless skinless chicken breast halves (about 1¼ lb)
¼ cup all-purpose flour
¼ cup butter or margarine
2 cloves garlic, finely chopped
1 cup dry white wine or chicken broth
2 tablespoons lemon juice
½ teaspoon pepper
1 tablespoon capers, if desired

1 Coat chicken with flour, shaking off excess.

2 Melt butter in 12-inch skillet over medium-high heat. Cook chicken and garlic in butter 15 to 20 minutes, turning chicken once, until juice of chicken is no longer pink when centers of thickest pieces are cut.

3 Add wine and lemon juice; sprinkle with pepper. Heat until hot. Sprinkle with capers.

It's worth a trip to the store to buy capers — they really add flavor to the dish.

1 Serving: Calories 300 (Calories from Fat 145); Total Fat 16g (Saturated Fat 8g); Cholesterol 105mg; Sodium 280mg; Total Carbohydrate 7g (Dietary Fiber 0g); Protein 28g

Italian White Beans with Chicken

Prep Time: 20 min ▪ Start to Finish: 20 min ▪ 4 Servings

1 tablespoon olive or vegetable oil
1 tablespoon chopped fresh or 1 teaspoon dried basil leaves
1 clove garlic, finely chopped
2 cups cut-up cooked chicken or turkey (about 1 lb)
1/2 cup chopped drained oil-packed sun-dried tomatoes
1/4 cup sliced ripe olives
2 cans (15 to 16 oz each) great northern beans, rinsed and drained

1 In 10-inch skillet, heat oil over medium heat. Cook basil and garlic in oil 3 minutes, stirring frequently.

2 Stir in remaining ingredients. Cook 5 to 7 minutes, stirring frequently, until hot.

Canned beans are so easy — no more hours of cooking to get great taste.

1 Serving: Calories 500 (Calories from Fat 110); Total Fat 12g (Saturated Fat 2.5g); Cholesterol 60mg; Sodium 180mg; Total Carbohydrate 57g (Dietary Fiber 14g); Protein 41g

Southwestern Chicken Scaloppine

Prep Time: 30 min ▪ Start to Finish: 30 min ▪ 4 Servings

4 boneless skinless chicken breast halves (about 1¹/₄ lb)

¹/₄ cup all-purpose flour

1 teaspoon ground cumin

¹/₄ teaspoon salt

2 tablespoons vegetable oil

¹/₄ cup chicken broth

¹/₄ teaspoon red pepper sauce, if desired

2 tablespoons lime juice

2 tablespoons chopped fresh cilantro

1 Between pieces of plastic wrap or waxed paper, place chicken breast half with smooth side down; gently pound with flat side of meat mallet or rolling pin until about ¹/₄ inch thick. Repeat with remaining chicken. Cut chicken into smaller pieces if desired.

2 In shallow dish, mix flour, cumin and salt. Coat chicken with flour mixture. Reserve 1 teaspoon flour mixture.

3 In 12-inch nonstick skillet, heat oil over medium heat. Add chicken; cook 3 to 5 minutes on each side or until golden brown and no longer pink in center. Remove chicken from skillet; cover to keep warm.

4 In small bowl, stir reserved 1 teaspoon flour mixture into broth. Gradually stir broth mixture and red pepper sauce into skillet. Heat to boiling; stir in lime juice and cilantro. Serve sauce over chicken.

1 Serving: Calories 260 (Calories from Fat 110); Total Fat 12g (Saturated Fat 2.5g); Cholesterol 85mg; Sodium 500mg; Total Carbohydrate 7g (Dietary Fiber 0g); Protein 33g

Caesar Chicken with Orzo

Prep Time: 30 min ■ Start to Finish: 30 min ■ 4 Servings

1 tablespoon vegetable oil
4 boneless skinless chicken breast halves (1¼ lb)
1 can (14½ oz) chicken broth
1 cup water
1 cup uncooked orzo pasta (6 oz)
1 bag (1 lb) frozen baby whole carrots, green beans and yellow beans
     (or other combination)
3 tablespoons Caesar dressing
⅛ teaspoon coarsely ground pepper

1 Heat oil in 10-inch skillet over medium-high heat. Cook chicken in oil about 10 minutes, turning once, until brown. Remove chicken from skillet; keep warm.

2 Add broth and water to skillet; heat to boiling. Stir in pasta; heat to boiling. Cook uncovered 8 to 10 minutes, stirring occasionally, until pasta is tender. Stir in frozen vegetables and dressing. Add chicken. Sprinkle with pepper.

3 Heat to boiling; reduce heat. Simmer uncovered about 5 minutes or until vegetables are crisp-tender and juice of chicken is no longer pink when centers of thickest pieces are cut.

Use your favorite combo of frozen vegetables here — the prep is so easy!

1 Serving: Calories 405 (Calories from Fat 115); Total Fat 13g (Saturated Fat 3g); Cholesterol 75mg; Sodium 670mg; Total Carbohydrate 43g (Dietary Fiber 6g); Protein 38g

Lemon Chicken with Olives

Prep Time: 10 min ◼ Start to Finish: 20 min ◼ 4 Servings

4 boneless skinless chicken breast halves (about 1½ lb)
1 tablespoon olive or canola oil
1 tablespoon lemon juice
1 teaspoon salt-free lemon-and-pepper seasoning
¼ cup sliced ripe olives
4 thin slices lemon

1 Set oven control to broil. Spray broiler pan rack with cooking spray. Starting at thickest edge of each chicken breast, cut horizontally almost to opposite side. Open cut chicken breast so it's an even thickness.

2 In small bowl, mix oil and lemon juice. Drizzle over both sides of chicken breasts. Sprinkle both sides with lemon-and-pepper seasoning. Place on rack in broiler pan.

3 Broil with tops 4 inches from heat about 10 minutes, turning once and topping with olives and lemon slices during last 2 minutes of broiling, until chicken is no longer pink in center.

1 Serving: Calories 210 (Calories from Fat 80); Total Fat 9g (Saturated Fat 2g); Cholesterol 85mg; Sodium 240mg; Total Carbohydrate 2g (Dietary Fiber 0g); Protein 31g

Spicy Chicken with Broccoli

Prep Time: 25 min ▪ Start to Finish: 25 min ▪ 4 Servings

4 boneless skinless chicken breasts
   (about 1 lb)
2 teaspoons cornstarch
1/2 teaspoon salt
1/4 teaspoon white pepper
1 lb fresh broccoli
3 green onions (with tops)
1 hot green chile or 1 teaspoon
   crushed red pepper flakes

3 tablespoons vegetable oil
2 tablespoons brown bean sauce,
   if desired
2 teaspoons finely chopped garlic
1 teaspoon sugar
1 teaspoon finely chopped gingerroot
1 tablespoon sesame seed, toasted

1 Cut chicken into 2×1/2-inch pieces. In medium bowl, toss chicken, cornstarch, salt and white pepper. (Black pepper can be used but, unlike white pepper, will add black specks.) Cover and refrigerate 20 minutes.

2 Meanwhile, peel broccoli stems. Cut broccoli lengthwise into 1-inch stems; remove florets. Cut stems diagonally into 1/4-inch slices.

3 In 1 1/2-quart saucepan, heat 3 cups water to boiling; add broccoli florets and stems. Cover and cook 1 minute; drain. Immediately rinse in cold water; drain.

4 Cut green onions diagonally into 1-inch pieces. Remove seeds and membrane from chile; cut chile into very thin slices.

5 Heat wok or 12-inch skillet until very hot. Add oil; rotate wok to coat side. Add chile, brown bean sauce, garlic, sugar and gingerroot; stir-fry 10 seconds. Add chicken; stir-fry about 2 minutes or until chicken is no longer pink in center. Add broccoli and green onions; stir-fry about 1 minute or until broccoli is hot. Sprinkle with sesame seed.

1 Serving: Calories 280 (Calories from Fat 140); Total Fat 15g (Saturated Fat 2.5g); Cholesterol 70mg; Sodium 380mg; Total Carbohydrate 9g (Dietary Fiber 3g); Protein 28g

Greek Turkey Burgers with Yogurt Sauce

Prep Time: 20 min ■ Start to Finish: 20 min ■ 4 Servings

Yogurt Sauce

1/2 cup plain fat-free yogurt

1/4 cup chopped red onion

1/4 cup chopped cucumber

Burgers

1 lb lean (at least 90%) ground turkey

1/2 cup plain fat-free yogurt

1 teaspoon dried oregano leaves

1/2 teaspoon garlic powder

1/2 teaspoon salt

1/2 teaspoon pepper

4 whole wheat hamburger buns

1 In small bowl, mix all sauce ingredients; refrigerate until ready to serve.

2 Set oven control to broil. In medium bowl, mix all burger ingredients except buns. Shape mixture into 4 patties, each about 1/2 inch thick and 5 inches in diameter. Place on rack in broiler pan.

3 Broil burgers with tops about 6 inches from heat 8 to 10 minutes, turning after 5 minutes, until thermometer inserted in center reads 165°F. Place burgers on buns. Serve with sauce.

Whole wheat buns are great, but it's OK if you want to use white buns or English muffins, whatever you like.

1 Serving: Calories 310 (Calories from Fat 70); Total Fat 8g (Saturated Fat 2g); Cholesterol 75mg; Sodium 640mg; Total Carbohydrate 26g (Dietary Fiber 3g); Protein 33g

Italian Steak Sandwiches

Prep Time: 20 min ▪ Start to Finish: 20 min ▪ 4 Sandwiches

1 tablespoon butter or margarine
1 medium onion, thinly sliced
4 beef cube steaks (about 1 1/2 lb)
1/2 teaspoon salt
1/4 teaspoon pepper
1/4 cup basil pesto
4 kaiser buns, split (toasted in oven if desired)
4 slices (about 3/4 oz each) mozzarella cheese
1 medium tomato, thinly sliced

1 In 12-inch nonstick skillet, melt butter over medium-high heat. Cook onion in butter 3 to 4 minutes, stirring frequently, until tender; push to side of skillet.

2 Add beef steaks to skillet; sprinkle with salt and pepper. Cook 5 to 8 minutes, turning once, for medium doneness (160°F).

3 Spread pesto on cut sides of buns. Layer steaks, cheese, onion and tomato in buns.

If you don't have the pesto on hand, you could use refrigerated spinach dip instead.

1 Sandwich: Calories 580 (Calories from Fat 270); Total Fat 30g (Saturated Fat 11g); Cholesterol 120mg; Sodium 930mg; Total Carbohydrate 32g (Dietary Fiber 3g); Protein 49g

Onion-Topped Caesar Burgers

Prep Time: 30 min ▪ Start to Finish: 30 min ▪ 4 Sandwiches

1 lb lean (at least 80%) ground beef

2 tablespoons chopped fresh parsley

$1/2$ cup Caesar dressing

$1/2$ teaspoon peppered seasoned salt

1 small sweet onion (such as Bermuda, Maui, Spanish or Walla Walla), cut into
    $1/4$- to $1/2$-inch slices

$1^1/2$ cups shredded romaine lettuce

2 tablespoons freshly shredded Parmesan cheese

4 sandwich buns, split

1 Heat coals or gas grill for direct heat. In medium bowl, mix beef, parsley, 2 tablespoons of the dressing and the peppered seasoned salt. Shape mixture into 4 patties, about $1/2$ inch thick.

2 Cover and grill patties over medium heat 10 to 12 minutes, turning once, until meat thermometer inserted in center reads 160°F and patties are no longer pink in center. Add onion slices for last 8 to 10 minutes of grilling, brushing with 2 tablespoons of the dressing and turning once, until crisp-tender.

3 In small bowl, toss romaine, remaining $1/4$ cup dressing and the cheese. Layer romaine, burger and onion in each bun.

1 Sandwich: Calories 500 (Calories from Fat 300); Total Fat 33g (Saturated Fat 9g); Cholesterol 75mg; Sodium 840mg; Total Carbohydrate 25g (Dietary Fiber 2g); Protein 26g

Mini Meat Loaves

Prep Time: 10 min ▪ Start to Finish: 30 min ▪ 6 Servings (2 loaves each)

$^1/_2$ cup ketchup

2 tablespoons packed brown sugar

1 lb lean (at least 80%) ground beef

$^1/_2$ lb ground pork

$^1/_2$ cup Original Bisquick® mix

$^1/_2$ teaspoon pepper

1 small onion, finely chopped ($^1/_4$ cup)

1 egg

1 Heat oven to 450°F. In small bowl, stir ketchup and brown sugar until mixed; reserve $^1/_4$ cup for topping. In large bowl, stir remaining ingredients and remaining ketchup mixture until well mixed.

2 Spray 13×9-inch pan with cooking spray. Place meat mixture in pan; pat into 12×4-inch rectangle. Cut lengthwise down center and then crosswise into sixths to form 12 loaves. Separate loaves, using spatula, so no edges are touching. Brush loaves with reserved $^1/_4$ cup ketchup mixture.

3 Bake 18 to 20 minutes or until loaves are no longer pink in center and meat thermometer inserted in center of loaves reads 160°F.

So cute! These little loaves bake much faster than the traditional loaf shape. Make that 30 minutes versus an hour or so!

1 Serving: Calories 300 (Calories from Fat 140); Total Fat 16g (Saturated Fat 6g); Cholesterol 105mg; Sodium 430mg; Total Carbohydrate 16g (Dietary Fiber 0g); Protein 22g

Filet of Beef with Mustard-Herb Crust

Prep Time: 30 min   Start to Finish: 1 hr   4 Servings

Crust

1 1/2 cups fine soft bread crumbs
    (about 3 slices bread)
1/4 cup olive oil
1/4 cup finely chopped fresh parsley
2 tablespoons finely chopped fresh mint leaves
1/2 teaspoon salt
1/2 teaspoon freshly ground pepper

Beef

4 center-cut beef filet mignons,
    1 3/4 inch thick (8 oz each)
Salt and pepper, if desired
1 tablespoon olive oil
1 tablespoon butter
3 tablespoons Dijon mustard

1 In small bowl, mix bread crumbs, 1/4 cup oil, the parsley, mint, 1/2 teaspoon salt and 1/2 teaspoon pepper; set aside.

2 Adjust oven rack so top of beef will be 4 to 6 inches from heat. Set oven control to broil.

3 Sprinkle beef with salt and pepper if desired. In 10-inch ovenproof skillet, heat 1 tablespoon oil and the butter over medium-high heat until butter is melted and no longer sizzles. Cook beef in oil mixture 5 minutes or until browned. Flip and cook 10 minutes longer or until brown and meat thermometer inserted in center of beef reads 145°F (medium-rare).

4 Divide mustard among beef, spreading evenly over tops. Spoon about 1/4 cup topping evenly over each filet. Use pancake turner to press down on topping so it sticks to filets. Broil 2 minutes or until bread crumbs are lightly browned.

5 Remove beef from oven and allow to stand 5 minutes before serving.

1 Serving: Calories 640 (Calories from Fat 330); Total Fat 36g (Saturated Fat 10g); Cholesterol 120mg; Sodium 1040mg; Total Carbohydrate 31g (Dietary Fiber 1g); Protein 48g

Orange Teriyaki Beef with Noodles

Prep Time: 20 min   Start to Finish: 20 min   4 Servings

1 lb beef boneless sirloin, cut into thin strips
1 can (14 oz) beef broth
¼ cup teriyaki stir-fry sauce
2 tablespoons orange marmalade
Dash of ground red pepper (cayenne)
1½ cups frozen snap pea pods (from 1-lb bag)
1½ cups uncooked fine egg noodles (3 oz)

1 Spray 12-inch skillet with cooking spray. Cook beef in skillet over medium-high heat 2 to 4 minutes, stirring occasionally, until brown. Remove beef from skillet; keep warm.

2 In same skillet, mix broth, stir-fry sauce, marmalade and red pepper. Heat to boiling. Stir in pea pods and noodles; reduce heat to medium. Cover and cook about 5 minutes or until noodles are tender.

3 Stir in beef. Cook uncovered 2 to 3 minutes or until sauce is slightly thickened.

1 Serving: Calories 270 (Calories from Fat 40); Total Fat 4.5g (Saturated Fat 1.5g); Cholesterol 80mg; Sodium 1190mg; Total Carbohydrate 27g (Dietary Fiber 2g); Protein 29g

Spanish Lamb and Couscous

Prep Time: 10 min ▪ Start to Finish: 30 min ▪ 4 Servings

4 lamb sirloin chops, $^1/_2$ inch thick (about 2 lb)
1 medium green bell pepper, chopped (1 cup)
$^1/_4$ cup chili sauce
1 can (14$^1/_2$ oz) diced tomatoes, undrained
$^1/_2$ teaspoon ground cumin
$^1/_2$ teaspoon dried marjoram leaves
$^1/_4$ teaspoon garlic powder
$^1/_4$ teaspoon salt
$^1/_4$ cup pitted ripe olives, cut in half
2 tablespoons chopped fresh parsley
2 cups hot cooked couscous

1 Spray 12-inch nonstick skillet with cooking spray; heat over medium heat. Cook lamb in skillet, turning once, until brown on both sides.

2 Stir in bell pepper, chili sauce, tomatoes, cumin, marjoram, garlic powder and salt; reduce heat to medium-low. Cover and simmer about 10 minutes or until lamb is light pink in center.

3 Stir in olives; sprinkle with parsley. Serve with couscous.

Couscous is so fast and easy — just pour on hot water and wait five minutes; it's an almost instant side dish.

1 Serving: Calories 310 (Calories from Fat 80); Total Fat 9g (Saturated Fat 3g); Cholesterol 70mg; Sodium 660mg; Total Carbohydrate 31g (Dietary Fiber 4g); Protein 27g

Breaded Pork Chops

Prep Time: 5 min ▪ Start to Finish: 15 min ▪ 8 Servings

1/2 cup Original Bisquick mix
12 saltine crackers, crushed (1/2 cup)
1 teaspoon seasoned salt
1/4 teaspoon pepper
1 egg or 1/4 cup fat-free egg product
2 tablespoons water
8 pork boneless loin chops, 1/2 inch thick (about 2 lb)
3 tablespoons vegetable oil

1 In shallow bowl, mix Bisquick mix, cracker crumbs, seasoned salt and pepper. In another shallow bowl, mix egg and water.

2 Dip pork into egg mixture, then coat with Bisquick mixture.

3 In 12-inch nonstick skillet, heat oil over medium-high heat. Cook pork in oil 10 to 12 minutes, turning once, until no longer pink in center.

1 Serving: Calories 270 (Calories from Fat 140); Total Fat 15g (Saturated Fat 4g); Cholesterol 90mg; Sodium 380mg; Total Carbohydrate 8g (Dietary Fiber 0g); Protein 24g

Pork Chops with Green Chile Corn

Prep Time: 20 min ▪ Start to Finish: 20 min ▪ 4 Servings

1 tablespoon vegetable oil
4 bone-in pork loin chops, $^3/_4$ inch thick (about $1^1/_2$ lb)
$^1/_2$ teaspoon seasoned salt
$^1/_2$ cup chopped red onion
$1^1/_2$ cups frozen whole kernel corn (from 1-lb bag)
1 can (4.5 oz) chopped green chiles, undrained
$^1/_4$ cup water
1 tablespoon Worcestershire sauce
$^1/_2$ teaspoon dried thyme leaves
1 medium tomato, seeded, chopped ($^3/_4$ cup)

1 In 12-inch nonstick skillet, heat oil over medium-high heat. Sprinkle pork chops with seasoned salt. Cook pork in oil 3 to 4 minutes or until brown on both sides. Remove pork from skillet.

2 Add onion, corn and green chiles to skillet. Cook 2 to 3 minutes over medium heat, stirring occasionally, just until mixture is thoroughly heated.

3 Stir in water, Worcestershire sauce and thyme. Place pork in skillet, pressing into vegetable mixture. Cover and cook 10 to 15 minutes, turning pork and stirring vegetables occasionally, until pork is no longer pink when cut near bone and meat thermometer reads 160°F.

4 Remove pork from skillet. Stir tomato into corn mixture; cook and stir 1 minute. Serve corn mixture with pork.

1 Serving: Calories 290 (Calories from Fat 120); Total Fat 13g (Saturated Fat 4g); Cholesterol 75mg; Sodium 380mg; Total Carbohydrate 17g (Dietary Fiber 2g); Protein 29g

Pork and White Bean Cassoulet

Prep Time: 30 min ▪ Start to Finish: 30 min ▪ 4 Servings

1/2 lb pork boneless loin, cut into 1/2-inch pieces
1 medium onion, chopped (1/2 cup)
1/4 teaspoon garlic powder
1/2 lb fully cooked kielbasa sausage, cut into 1/4-inch slices
1 can (14 1/2 oz) stewed tomatoes, undrained
1/4 cup chili sauce or ketchup
1 tablespoon chopped fresh or 1/4 teaspoon dried thyme leaves
1 cup frozen cut green beans
1 can (15 to 16 oz) great northern beans, drained
2 tablespoons chopped fresh parsley

1 Spray 12-inch nonstick skillet with cooking spray; heat over medium heat. Cook pork, onion and garlic powder in skillet 3 to 4 minutes, stirring occasionally, until pork is brown.

2 Stir in kielbasa, tomatoes, chili sauce, thyme and frozen green beans. Heat to boiling over medium heat. Cover and boil 5 minutes, stirring occasionally.

3 Stir in great northern beans. Cover and cook 8 to 10 minutes, stirring occasionally, until green beans are tender. Sprinkle with parsley.

Want to make this even faster? Cut the meats and onion the night before or in the morning; wrap tightly and refrigerate until you make the cassoulet.

1 Serving: Calories 460 (Calories from Fat 190); Total Fat 21g (Saturated Fat 7g); Cholesterol 70mg; Sodium 1090mg; Total Carbohydrate 44g (Dietary Fiber 9g); Protein 32g

Cajun Pork Burgers

Prep Time: 25 min ▪ Start to Finish: 25 min ▪ 4 Sandwiches

1 tablespoon olive or vegetable oil
1½ cups frozen bell pepper and onion stir-fry (from 1-lb bag)
1 medium stalk celery, sliced (½ cup)
2 tablespoons chopped fresh parsley
1 lb ground pork
2 tablespoons chili sauce
½ teaspoon garlic salt
¼ teaspoon dried thyme leaves
⅛ teaspoon ground red pepper (cayenne)
4 sandwich buns

1 Heat oven to 375°F. Heat oil in 10-inch nonstick skillet over medium-high heat. Cook frozen bell pepper mixture and celery in oil 3 to 4 minutes, stirring occasionally, until tender. Stir in parsley; remove from skillet. Cover to keep warm.

2 Mix pork, chili sauce, garlic salt, thyme and red pepper. Shape mixture into 4 oval patties, ½ inch thick. Cook patties in hot skillet over medium heat 8 to 10 minutes, turning once, until no longer pink in center.

3 Place buns, cut sides up, on ungreased cookie sheet. Bake 3 to 5 minutes or until toasted. Serve patties on buns topped with vegetables.

1 Sandwich: Calories 370 (Calories from Fat 190); Total Fat 21g (Saturated Fat 7g); Cholesterol 70mg; Sodium 470mg; Total Carbohydrate 24g (Dietary Fiber 2g); Protein 24g

Pork Lo Mein

Prep Time: 25 min ▪ Start to Finish: 25 min ▪ 4 servings

¹/₂ lb boneless pork loin

2¹/₂ cups sugar snap pea pods

1¹/₂ cups ready-to-eat baby-cut carrots, cut lengthwise into ¹/₄-inch sticks

¹/₂ package (9-oz size) refrigerated linguine, cut into 2-inch pieces

¹/₃ cup chicken broth

1 tablespoon soy sauce

2 teaspoons cornstarch

1 teaspoon sugar

2 teaspoons finely chopped gingerroot

2 to 4 cloves garlic, finely chopped

2 teaspoons canola oil

¹/₂ cup thinly sliced red onion

Toasted sesame seed, if desired*

1 Trim fat from pork. Cut pork with grain into 2×1-inch strips; cut strips across grain into ¹/₈-inch slices (pork is easier to cut if partially frozen, about 1¹/₂ hours). Remove strings from pea pods.

2 In 3-quart saucepan, heat 2 quarts water to boiling. Add pea pods, carrots and linguine; heat to boiling. Boil 2 to 3 minutes or just until linguine is tender; drain.

3 In small bowl, mix broth, soy sauce, cornstarch, sugar, gingerroot and garlic.

4 In 12-inch nonstick skillet or wok, heat oil over medium-high heat. Add pork and onion; stir-fry about 2 minutes or until pork is no longer pink. Stir broth mixture; stir into pork mixture. Stir in pea pods, carrots and linguine. Cook 2 minutes, stirring occasionally. Sprinkle with sesame seed.

*To toast sesame seed, sprinkle in an ungreased heavy skillet and cook over medium-low heat 5 to 7 minutes, stirring frequently until browning begins, then stirring constantly until golden brown.

1 Serving: Calories 200 (Calories from Fat 45); Total Fat 5g (Saturated Fat 1g); Cholesterol 35mg; Sodium 370mg; Total Carbohydrate 21g (Dietary Fiber 4g); Protein 17g

Cooking the vegetables
with the linguine saves time —
and pans!

Manhattan Clam Chowder

Lobster Bisque

Salmon Burgers with Sour Cream–Dill Sauce

Lemon and Herb Salmon Packets

Salmon with Soy-Ginger Sauce

Tuna with Mediterranean Vegetables

Garlic- and Herb-Broiled Rainbow Trout

Sole Fillets with Spinach

Cuban-Style Tilapia Salad

Graham-Crusted Tilapia

Snapper with Sautéed Tomato-Pepper Sauce

Crispy Baked Catfish

Beer Batter-Fried Fish

Lemon-Pepper Fish Fillet Sandwiches

Pecan-Crusted Fish Fillets

Creamy Crab au Gratin

Linguine with Red Clam Sauce

Ramen Shrimp and Vegetables

Scampi with Fettuccine

4

from the sea

Manhattan Clam Chowder

Prep Time: 30 min ▪ Start to Finish: 40 min ▪ 4 Servings

$1/4$ cup finely chopped bacon or salt pork
1 small onion, finely chopped ($1/4$ cup)
2 cans (6.5 oz each) minced or whole clams, undrained*
2 medium potatoes, diced (2 cups)
$1/3$ cup chopped celery
1 cup water
2 teaspoons chopped fresh parsley
1 teaspoon chopped fresh or $1/4$ teaspoon dried thyme leaves
$1/4$ teaspoon salt
$1/8$ teaspoon pepper
1 can (14.5 oz) whole tomatoes, undrained

1 In 4-quart Dutch oven, cook bacon and onion over medium heat 8 to 10 minutes, stirring occasionally, until bacon is crisp and onion is tender; drain off fat.

2 Stir in clams, potatoes, celery and water. Heat to boiling; reduce heat. Cover and simmer about 10 minutes or until potatoes are tender.

3 Stir in remaining ingredients, breaking up tomatoes with a fork. Heat to boiling, stirring occasionally.

* 1 pint shucked fresh clams with their liquid can be substituted for the canned clams. Chop clams and stir in with the potatoes in step 2.

1 Serving: Calories 230 (Calories from Fat 25); Total Fat 3g (Saturated Fat 0.5g); Cholesterol 65mg; Sodium 450mg; Total Carbohydrate 23g (Dietary Fiber 3g); Protein 26g

Lobster Bisque

Prep Time: 25 min ▪ Start to Finish: 25 min ▪ 4 Servings

3 tablespoons butter or margarine
1 small onion, finely chopped ($1/4$ cup)
3 tablespoons all-purpose flour
1 tablespoon chopped fresh parsley
$1/2$ teaspoon salt
$1/8$ teaspoon pepper
2 cups milk
1 cup chicken broth
$11/4$ cups chopped fresh or frozen (thawed) lobster (about 12 oz)

1 Melt butter in 3-quart saucepan over low heat. Cook onion in butter, stirring occasionally, until tender. Stir in flour, parsley, salt and pepper. Cook, stirring constantly, until mixture is bubbly; remove from heat.

2 Stir in milk and broth. Heat to boiling, stirring constantly. Boil and stir 1 minute. Stir in lobster. Heat to boiling; reduce heat. Simmer about 3 minutes, stirring frequently, until lobster is white.

Have a favorite fish other than lobster? Use that instead. Halibut, orange roughy or haddock make good substitutions.

1 Serving: Calories 205 (Calories from Fat 100); Total Fat 11g (Saturated Fat 7g); Cholesterol 65mg; Sodium 590mg; Total Carbohydrate 12g (Dietary Fiber 0g); Protein 14g

Salmon Burgers with Sour Cream–Dill Sauce

Prep Time: 30 min ▪ Start to Finish: 30min ▪ 4 Servings

Sour Cream–Dill Sauce

1/3 cup sour cream

3 tablespoons mayonnaise or salad dressing

3/4 teaspoon dried dill weed

Salmon Burgers

1 large egg

2 tablespoons milk

1 can (14 3/4 oz) red or pink salmon, drained, skin and bones removed and salmon flaked

2 medium green onions, chopped (2 tablespoons)

1 cup soft bread crumbs (about 1 1/2 slices bread)

1/4 teaspoon salt

1 tablespoon vegetable oil

1 In small bowl, stir all sauce ingredients until well mixed; refrigerate until serving.

2 In medium bowl, beat egg and milk with fork or wire whisk. Stir in remaining ingredients except oil. Shape mixture into 4 patties, about 4 inches in diameter.

3 In 10-inch nonstick skillet, heat oil over medium heat. Cook patties in oil about 8 minutes, turning once, until golden brown. Serve with sauce.

1 Serving: Calories 300 (Calories from Fat 200); Total Fat 22g (Saturated Fat 6g); Cholesterol 120mg; Sodium 750mg; Total Carbohydrate 6g (Dietary Fiber 0g); Protein 20g

Lemon and Herb Salmon Packets

Prep Time: 30 min ▪ Start to Finish: 30 min ▪ 4 Servings

2 cups uncooked instant rice
1 can (14 oz) fat-free or low sodium chicken broth
1 cup matchstick-cut carrots (from 10-oz bag)
4 salmon fillets (4 to 6 oz each)
1 teaspoon lemon pepper seasoning salt
1/3 cup chopped fresh chives
1 medium lemon, cut lengthwise in half, then cut crosswise into 1/4-inch slices

1 Heat coals or gas grill for direct heat. Spray four 18×12-inch sheets of heavy-duty aluminum foil with cooking spray.

2 Mix rice and broth in medium bowl. Let stand about 5 minutes or until most of broth is absorbed. Stir in carrots.

3 Place salmon fillet on center of each foil sheet. Sprinkle with lemon pepper seasoning salt; top with chives. Arrange lemon slices over salmon. Spoon rice mixture around each fillet. Fold foil over salmon and rice so edges meet. Seal edges, making tight 1/2-inch fold; fold again. Allow space on sides for circulation and expansion.

4 Cover and grill packets 4 to 6 inches from low heat 11 to 14 minutes or until salmon flakes easily with fork. Place packets on plates. Cut large X across top of each packet; carefully fold back foil to allow steam to escape.

1 Serving: Calories 400 (Calories from Fat 70); Total Fat 8g (Saturated Fat 2g); Cholesterol 75mg; Sodium 870mg; Total Carbohydrate 51g (Dietary Fiber 2g); Protein 31g

Salmon with Soy-Ginger Sauce

Prep Time: 10 min ▪ Start to Finish: 25 min ▪ 4 Servings

Salmon
2 tablespoons olive oil
4 salmon steaks, about ³/₄ inch thick (2 lb)

Soy-Ginger Sauce
¹/₄ cup plus 2 tablespoons soy sauce
¹/₄ cup mirin (sweet rice wine) or apple juice
2 tablespoons lime juice
2 tablespoons water
1 tablespoon honey
1 tablespoon grated gingerroot

1 In 10-inch skillet (preferably nonstick), heat oil over medium-high heat until shimmering and hot. Add salmon and cook 3 minutes or until brown on one side. Flip and brown other side, about 3 minutes longer.

2 In small bowl, mix all sauce ingredients. Add mixture to skillet. Reduce heat to medium-low.

3 Cover and cook 8 to 12 minutes or until salmon flakes easily with fork. Place salmon on serving plates and drizzle with sauce.

1 Serving: Calories 370 (Calories from Fat 160); Total Fat 18g (Saturated Fat 4g); Cholesterol 125mg; Sodium 1480mg; Total Carbohydrate 9g (Dietary Fiber 0g); Protein 42g

Tuna with Mediterranean Vegetables

Prep Time: 20 min ▪ Start to Finish: 20 min ▪ 6 Servings

1 tablespoon olive or canola oil

3 cloves garlic, finely chopped

2 cups sliced fresh mushrooms

2 medium yellow summer squash or zucchini, cut into $1/4$-inch slices (3 cups)

1 cup cherry tomatoes, cut in half

$1/4$ cup sliced ripe olives

1 tablespoon chopped fresh or 1 teaspoon dried basil leaves

$1/2$ teaspoon salt

$1/4$ teaspoon pepper

1 tablespoon olive or canola oil

6 tuna steaks, $1/2$ inch thick (5 oz each)

1 tablespoon chopped fresh or 1 teaspoon dried oregano leaves

1 In 12-inch nonstick skillet, heat 1 tablespoon oil over medium-high heat. Cook garlic, mushrooms and squash in oil 2 to 3 minutes, stirring frequently. Stir in tomatoes, olives, basil, salt and pepper. Cook 2 to 4 minutes, stirring frequently, until vegetables are tender. Remove from heat; cover to keep warm.

2 Brush grill rack with oil. Heat coals or gas grill for direct heat. Rub 1 tablespoon oil over both sides of tuna steaks. Cover and grill tuna over medium heat 2 minutes; turn. Sprinkle tuna with oregano. Cover and grill 1 to 3 minutes longer or until tuna flakes easily with fork and is slightly pink in center. Serve tuna with vegetables.

1 Serving: Calories 250 (Calories from Fat 110); Total Fat 13g (Saturated Fat 3g); Cholesterol 85mg; Sodium 330mg; Total Carbohydrate 6g (Dietary Fiber 2g); Protein 29g

Garlic- and Herb-Broiled Rainbow Trout

Prep Time: 15 min ▮ Start to Finish: 15 min ▮ 4 Servings

4 rainbow trout or other medium-firm fish fillets, $1/4$ to $1/2$ inch thick (about 1 lb)

2 tablespoons lime or lemon juice

$2/3$ cup soft bread crumbs (about 1 slice bread)

1 teaspoon Italian seasoning

2 teaspoons canola or soybean oil

$1/2$ teaspoon garlic powder

$1/4$ teaspoon pepper

1 Set oven control to broil. Spray broiler pan rack with cooking spray. Place fish on rack in broiler pan. Brush with lime juice. Broil with tops about 4 inches from heat 3 minutes.

2 While fish is broiling, mix remaining ingredients.

3 Spoon bread crumb mixture on top of fish. Broil about 1 minute longer or until fish flakes easily with fork.

No soybean or canola oil? Just use olive oil.

1 Serving: Calories 180 (Calories from Fat 70); Total Fat 8g (Saturated Fat 2g); Cholesterol 65mg; Sodium 95mg; Total Carbohydrate 4g (Dietary Fiber 0g); Protein 22g

Sole Fillets with Spinach

Prep Time: 25 min ▪ Start to Finish: 25 min ▪ 4 Servings

1 lb spinach
1 teaspoon poultry seasoning
$^1/_2$ teaspoon chili powder
$^1/_2$ teaspoon salt
1 to 1$^1/_2$ lb sole, flounder or red snapper fillets, $^1/_4$ to $^1/_2$ inch thick
2 tablespoons butter or margarine, melted
Lemon wedges

1 Heat coals or gas grill for direct heat. Spray 13×9-inch aluminum foil pan with cooking spray. Rinse spinach; shake off excess water, but do not dry. Place about three-fourths of the spinach leaves in pan, covering bottom completely.

2 Mix poultry seasoning, chili powder and salt. Lightly rub into both sides of fish. Place fish on spinach, folding thin tail ends under and, if necessary, overlapping thin edges slightly. Drizzle with butter. Cover fish completely with remaining spinach.

3 Cover and grill fish and spinach 4 inches from medium heat 8 to 10 minutes or until fish flakes easily with fork. Check after about 3 minutes; if top layer of spinach is charring, sprinkle with about $^1/_4$ cup water. Serve fish and spinach from pan with a slotted spoon. Serve with lemon wedges.

Is it done yet? Save time by knowing when the fish is ready to serve. To test fish for doneness, place a fork in the thickest part and gently twist. The fish will flake easily when it's cooked through.

1 Serving: Calories 150 (Calories from Fat 65); Total Fat 7g (Saturated Fat 4g); Cholesterol 70mg; Sodium 580mg; Total Carbohydrate 3g (Dietary Fiber 2g); Protein 21g

Cuban-Style Tilapia Salad

Prep Time: 30 min ▪ Start to Finish: 30 min ▪ 4 Servings

Dressing

1/2 cup pineapple juice

1 teaspoon grated lime peel

2 tablespoons lime juice

1 tablespoon canola oil

1/4 teaspoon seasoned salt

Tilapia Salad

4 tilapia or other mild-flavored white fish fillets (about 5 oz each)

Cooking spray

2 tablespoons lime juice

1/2 teaspoon seasoned salt

4 cups mixed salad greens

2 cups fresh or canned (drained) pineapple chunks

1/4 cup fresh mint leaves

1 In 1-cup glass measuring cup, beat all dressing ingredients with wire whisk.

2 Set oven control to broil. On rack in broiler pan, place fish; spray tops of fish with cooking spray. Sprinkle tops of fish with 2 tablespoons lime juice and the seasoned salt. Broil with tops 4 to 6 inches from heat 6 to 8 minutes or until fish flakes easily with fork.

3 Meanwhile, on each of 4 plates, arrange 1 cup salad greens. Divide pineapple among plates. Place fish on or next to greens. Sprinkle greens and fish with mint. Serve with dressing.

1 Serving: Calories 230 (Calories from Fat 50); Total Fat 5g (Saturated Fat 0.5g); Cholesterol 75mg; Sodium 390mg; Total Carbohydrate 17g (Dietary Fiber 2g); Protein 28g

Graham-Crusted Tilapia

Prep Time: 15 min ▪ Start to Finish: 25 min ▪ 4 Servings

1 lb tilapia, cod, haddock or other medium-firm fish fillets, about ³/₄ inch thick
¹/₂ cup graham cracker crumbs (about 8 squares)
1 teaspoon grated lemon peel
¹/₄ teaspoon salt
¹/₈ teaspoon pepper
¹/₄ cup milk
2 tablespoons canola or soybean oil
2 tablespoons chopped toasted pecans*

1 Move oven rack to position slightly above middle of oven. Heat oven to 500°F.

2 Cut fish fillets crosswise into 2-inch-wide pieces. Mix cracker crumbs, lemon peel, salt and pepper in shallow dish. Place milk in another shallow dish.

3 Dip fish into milk, then coat with cracker mixture; place in ungreased rectangular pan, 13×9×2 inches. Drizzle oil over fish; sprinkle with pecans.

4 Bake uncovered about 10 minutes or until fish flakes easily with fork.

*To toast nuts, bake uncovered in ungreased shallow pan in 350°F oven about 10 minutes, stirring occasionally, until golden brown.

Here's a great new use for graham crackers!

1 Serving: Calories 230 (Calories from Fat 110); Total Fat 12g (Saturated Fat 1.5g); Cholesterol 60mg; Sodium 310mg; Total Carbohydrate 9g (Dietary Fiber 0g); Protein 23g

Snapper with Sautéed Tomato-Pepper Sauce

Prep Time: 20 min ▪ Start to Finish: 20 min ▪ 4 Servings

1 lb red snapper, cod or other medium-firm fish fillets ($\frac{1}{2}$ inch thick)
1 large tomato, chopped (1 cup)
1 small green bell pepper, chopped ($\frac{1}{2}$ cup)
1 small onion, sliced
2 tablespoons finely chopped fresh cilantro or parsley
$\frac{1}{4}$ teaspoon salt
$\frac{1}{4}$ cup dry white wine or chicken broth

1 If fish fillets are large, cut into 4 serving pieces. Heat 10-inch nonstick skillet over medium heat.

2 Arrange fish, skin sides down, in single layer in skillet. Cook uncovered 4 to 6 minutes, turning once, until fish flakes easily with fork. Remove fish to warm platter; keep warm.

3 In same skillet, cook remaining ingredients except wine over medium heat 3 to 5 minutes, stirring frequently, until bell pepper and onion are crisp-tender. Stir in wine; cook about 1 minute or until hot. Spoon tomato mixture over fish.

Use any color bell pepper you want — red, yellow or orange will give you a slightly sweeter sauce.

1 Serving: Calories 115 (Calories from Fat 10); Total Fat 1g (Saturated Fat 0g); Cholesterol 50mg; Sodium 230mg; Total Carbohydrate 5g (Dietary Fiber 1g); Protein 19g

Crispy Baked Catfish

Prep Time: 15 min ▪ Start to Finish: 30 min ▪ 4 Servings

1 lb catfish, flounder or other delicate-texture fish fillets
1/4 cup yellow cornmeal
1/4 cup dry bread crumbs
1 teaspoon chili powder
1/4 teaspoon paprika
1/2 teaspoon garlic salt
1/4 teaspoon pepper
1/4 cup French or ranch dressing

1 Heat oven to 450°F. Spray broiler pan rack with cooking spray. If fish fillets are large, cut into 4 serving pieces.

2 Mix cornmeal, bread crumbs, chili powder, paprika, garlic salt and pepper. Lightly brush dressing on all sides of fish. Coat fish with cornmeal mixture.

3 Place fish on rack in broiler pan. Bake uncovered 15 to 18 minutes or until fish flakes easily with fork.

Save some time by using 1/2 cup of a purchased seasoned fish coating mix instead of preparing the coating mixture yourself.

1 Serving: Calories 235 (Calories from Fat 70); Total Fat 8g (Saturated Fat 1g); Cholesterol 75mg; Sodium 450mg; Total Carbohydrate 14g (Dietary Fiber 1g); Protein 28g

Beer Batter-Fried Fish

Prep Time: 25 min ▪ Start to Finish: 25 min ▪ 4 Servings

Vegetable oil

1 lb walleye, sole or other delicate- to medium-texture fish fillets,
    about 3/4 inch thick

3 to 4 tablespoons mix

1 cup Original Bisquick mix

1/2 cup regular or nonalcoholic beer

1 large egg

1/2 teaspoon salt

Tartar sauce, if desired

1 In 4-quart Dutch oven or deep fryer, heat oil (1 1/2 inches) to 350°F. Cut fish into 8 serving pieces. Lightly coat fish with 3 to 4 tablespoons Bisquick mix.

2 In medium bowl, mix remaining ingredients except tartar sauce with hand beater until smooth. (If batter is too thick, stir in additional beer, 1 tablespoon at a time, until desired consistency.) Dip fish into batter, letting excess drip into bowl.

3 Fry batches of fish in oil about 4 minutes, turning once, until golden brown. Remove with slotted spoon; drain on paper towels. Serve hot with tartar sauce.

Add some French fries, and you'll have the classic fish and chips.

1 Serving: Calories 280 (Calories from Fat 100); Total Fat 11g (Saturated Fat 2.5g); Cholesterol 100mg; Sodium 710mg; Total Carbohydrate 20g (Dietary Fiber 0g); Protein 25g

Lemon-Pepper Fish Fillet Sandwiches

Prep Time: 15 min ▪ Start to Finish: 15 min ▪ 4 Sandwiches

2 tablespoons yellow cornmeal
2 tablespoons all-purpose flour
1 teaspoon seasoned salt
$1/2$ teaspoon lemon-pepper seasoning
1 tablespoon vegetable oil
2 walleye (about 6 oz each) or other delicate- to medium-texture fish fillets like sole or white fish, each cut crosswise in half
$1/4$ cup tartar sauce
4 whole-grain or rye sandwich buns, toasted
1 cup shredded lettuce

1 In shallow bowl, mix cornmeal, flour, seasoned salt and lemon-pepper seasoning.

2 In 12-inch nonstick skillet, heat oil over medium-high heat. Coat fish fillets with flour mixture. Cook in oil 4 to 6 minutes, turning once, until fish flakes easily with fork.

3 Spread tartar sauce on cut sides of toasted buns. Layer lettuce and fish fillets in buns.

1 Sandwich: Calories 310 (Calories from Fat 130); Total Fat 14g (Saturated Fat 2g); Cholesterol 55mg; Sodium 870mg; Total Carbohydrate 25g (Dietary Fiber 2g); Protein 21g

Pecan-Crusted Fish Fillets

Prep Time: 25 min ▪ Start to Finish: 25 min ▪ 4 Servings

1 cup finely chopped pecans (not ground)
1/4 cup dry bread crumbs
2 teaspoons grated lemon peel
1 large egg
1 tablespoon milk
1 lb sole, orange roughy, walleye or other delicate- to medium-texture fish fillets,
  about 1/2 inch thick
1/2 teaspoon salt
1/4 teaspoon pepper
2 tablespoons vegetable oil
Lemon wedges

1 In shallow dish, mix pecans, bread crumbs and lemon peel. In small bowl, beat egg and milk with fork or wire whisk until blended.

2 Cut fish into 4 serving pieces. Sprinkle both sides of fish with salt and pepper. Coat fish with egg mixture, then coat well with pecan mixture, pressing lightly into fish.

3 In 12-inch nonstick skillet, heat oil over medium heat. Add fish. Reduce heat to medium-low. Cook 6 to 10 minutes, carefully turning once with 2 pancake turners, until fish flakes easily with fork and is brown. Serve with lemon wedges.

1 Serving: Calories 350 (Calories from Fat 220); Total Fat 25g (Saturated Fat 3g); Cholesterol 105mg; Sodium 450mg; Total Carbohydrate 9g (Dietary Fiber 3g); Protein 24g

Creamy Crab au Gratin

Prep Time: 15 min ▪ Start to Finish: 30 min ▪ 4 Servings

2 tablespoons butter or margarine
1½ cups sliced mushrooms (4 oz)
2 medium stalks celery, sliced (1 cup)
1 can (14 oz) chicken broth
¾ cup half-and-half
3 tablespoons all-purpose flour
½ teaspoon red pepper sauce
2 packages (8 oz each) refrigerated imitation crabmeat chunks or 2 cups
    chopped cooked crabmeat
1 cup soft bread crumbs (about 1½ slices bread)

1 Heat oven to 400°F. Spray rectangular baking dish, 11×7×1½ inches, with cooking spray. Melt butter in 10-inch skillet over medium-high heat. Cook mushrooms and celery in butter about 4 minutes, stirring frequently, until celery is tender. Stir in broth. Heat to boiling; reduce heat to medium.

2 Beat half-and-half, flour and pepper sauce with wire whisk until smooth; stir into vegetable mixture. Heat to boiling, stirring constantly. Boil and stir 1 minute. Stir in crabmeat.

3 Spoon crabmeat mixture into baking dish. Top with bread crumbs. Bake uncovered about 15 minutes or until heated through.

Fresh mushrooms are available already sliced — it's a great time-saver! If you happen to have only whole ones around, here's a speedy slicing secret: Use an egg slicer — it works great for mushrooms, too!

1 Serving: Calories 285 (Calories from Fat 45); Total Fat 12g (Saturated Fat 6g); Cholesterol 60mg; Sodium 1580mg; Total Carbohydrate 22g (Dietary Fiber 1g); Protein 23g

Linguine with Red Clam Sauce

Prep Time: 40 min ▪ Start to Finish: 1 hr ▪ 6 Servings

Red Clam Sauce
1 pint shucked fresh small clams, drained and liquor reserved*
1/4 cup olive or vegetable oil
3 cloves garlic, finely chopped
1 can (28 oz) Italian-style (plum) tomatoes, drained and chopped
1 small jalapeño chili, seeded and finely chopped
1 tablespoon chopped fresh parsley
1 teaspoon salt

Linguine
8 ounces uncooked linguine
Garnish
Chopped fresh parsley

1 Chop clams; set aside. In 3-quart saucepan, heat oil over medium-high heat. Cook garlic in oil, stirring frequently, until golden. Stir in tomatoes and chili. Cook 3 minutes, stirring frequently. Stir in clam liquor. Heat to boiling; reduce heat. Simmer uncovered 10 minutes. Stir in clams, parsley and salt. Cover and simmer about 15 minutes, stirring occasionally, until clams are tender.

2 Meanwhile, cook linguine as directed on package. Drain and keep warm.

3 In large bowl, toss linguine and sauce. Sprinkle with parsley.

* 2 cans (6.5 oz each) minced clams, undrained, can be substituted for the fresh clams. Decrease simmer time to 5 minutes.

1 Serving: Calories 300 (Calories from Fat 90); Total Fat 10g (Saturated Fat 1.5g); Cholesterol 15mg; Sodium 620mg; Total Carbohydrate 38g (Dietary Fiber 4g); Protein 13g

Ramen Shrimp and Vegetables

Prep Time: 20 min ▪ Start to Finish: 20 min ▪ 4 Servings

1 lb uncooked peeled deveined medium shrimp, thawed if frozen and tails peeled
2 cups water
1 package (3 oz) Oriental-flavor ramen noodle soup mix
1 bag (1 lb) fresh stir-fry vegetables
¼ cup stir-fry sauce

1 Heat 12-inch nonstick skillet over medium-high heat. Cook shrimp in skillet 2 to 4 minutes, stirring occasionally, until pink and firm. Remove shrimp from skillet; keep warm.

2 Heat water to boiling in same skillet. Break up noodles from soup mix into water; stir until slightly softened. Stir in vegetables.

3 Heat to boiling. Boil 4 to 6 minutes, stirring occasionally, until vegetables are crisp-tender. Stir in seasoning packet from soup mix and stir-fry sauce. Cook 3 to 5 minutes, stirring frequently, until hot. Stir in shrimp.

Not in the mood for shrimp? Substitute 1 pound beef strips for stir-fry for the shrimp. Cook the beef in a heated skillet sprayed with cooking oil for 3 to 5 minutes, stirring occasionally, until brown.

1 Serving: Calories 210 (Calories from Fat 40); Total Fat 4.5g (Saturated Fat 1g); Cholesterol 160mg; Sodium 1160mg; Total Carbohydrate 21g (Dietary Fiber 3g); Protein 22g

Scampi with Fettuccine

Prep Time: 20 min ▪ Start to Finish: 20 min ▪ 4 Servings

8 oz uncooked fettuccine

2 tablespoons olive or vegetable oil

1¹/₂ lb uncooked deveined peeled medium shrimp, thawed if frozen,
    tail shells removed

2 medium green onions, thinly sliced (2 tablespoons)

2 cloves garlic, finely chopped

1 tablespoon chopped fresh or ¹/₂ teaspoon dried basil leaves

1 tablespoon chopped fresh parsley

2 tablespoons lemon juice

¹/₄ teaspoon salt

1 Cook and drain fettuccine as directed on package.

2 In 10-inch skillet, heat oil over medium heat. Cook remaining ingredients in oil 2 to 3 minutes, stirring frequently, until shrimp are pink; remove from heat.

3 Toss fettuccine with shrimp mixture in skillet.

Peeling and deveining shrimp is time consuming — and unnecessary! Luckily for us, somebody else has done this laborious task. Look for fresh or frozen shrimp that has already been peeled and deveined.

1 Serving: Calories 380 (Calories from Fat 90); Total Fat 10g (Saturated Fat 1.5g); Cholesterol 290mg; Sodium 670mg; Total Carbohydrate 38g (Dietary Fiber 2g); Protein 33g

Five-Layer Mexican Dip

Lime Tortilla Chips

Super Chicken Nachos

Cheesy Chicken Quesadillas

Chicken Tostadas

Chorizo Burritos

Salsa-Rice Burritos

South-of-the-Border Burritos

Grilled Fish Tacos

Turkey Soft Tacos

Three-Bean Enchilada Chili

Beef Fajita Bowls

Mexican Beef and Black Beans

Sweet-and-Spicy Beef Fajitas

Fajita Pizza

5

mexican night

Five-Layer Mexican Dip

Prep Time: 20 min ▪ Start to Finish: 20 min ▪ 16 Servings

1 can (15 to 16 oz) refried beans
2 tablespoons salsa
1½ cups sour cream
1 cup guacamole
1 cup shredded Cheddar cheese (4 oz)
2 medium green onions, chopped (2 tablespoons)
Tortilla chips, if desired

1 Mix refried beans and salsa. Spread in thin layer on 12- or 13-inch serving plate or pizza pan.

2 Spread sour cream over beans, leaving about 1-inch border of beans around edge. Spread guacamole over sour cream, leaving border of sour cream showing.

3 Sprinkle cheese over guacamole. Sprinkle onions over cheese. Serve immediately, or cover and refrigerate until serving. Serve with tortilla chips.

Save time and buy guacamole. It's in the dairy or frozen section of the supermarket and may be labeled "avocado dip" instead of "guacamole."

1 Serving: Calories 120 (Calories from Fat 80); Total Fat 9g (Saturated Fat 5g); Cholesterol 25mg; Sodium 220mg; Total Carbohydrate 8g (Dietary Fiber 2g); Protein 4g

Lime Tortilla Chips

Prep Time: 10 min ▪ Start to Finish: 20 min ▪ 6 Servings (8 chips each)

$^1/_2$ teaspoon grated lime peel
2 tablespoons lime juice
2 teaspoons olive or vegetable oil
2 teaspoons honey
Dash of salt
4 flour tortillas (8 inch)
Salsa, if desired

1 Heat oven to 350°F. Spray large cookie sheet with cooking spray. Mix all ingredients except tortillas. Brush lime mixture on both sides of each tortilla. Cut each tortilla into 12 wedges. Place in single layer on cookie sheet.

2 Bake 8 to 10 minutes or until crisp and light golden brown; cool. Serve with salsa. Store remaining chips in airtight container at room temperature.

1 Serving: Calories 115 (Calories from Fat 35); Total Fat 4g (Saturated Fat 1g); Cholesterol 0mg; Sodium 140mg; Total Carbohydrate 18g (Dietary Fiber 1g); Protein 3g

Super Chicken Nachos

Prep Time: 10 min ▪ Start to Finish: 15 min ▪ 6 Servings

6 oz tortilla chips
$\frac{1}{2}$ cup chopped ripe avocado
$\frac{1}{2}$ teaspoon ground cumin
1 large tomato, seeded, chopped (1 cup)
1 cup shredded cooked chicken
1 cup shredded Monterey Jack cheese (4 oz)
Salsa and sour cream, if desired

1 Heat oven to 400°F. Line cookie sheet with foil. Place tortilla chips on cookie sheet. In small bowl, mix avocado, cumin and tomato; spoon over chips. Top with chicken and cheese.

2 Bake 3 to 5 minutes or until cheese is melted. Serve with salsa and sour cream.

1 Serving: Calories 280 (Calories from Fat 150); Total Fat 16g (Saturated Fat 5g); Cholesterol 35mg; Sodium 290mg; Total Carbohydrate 20g (Dietary Fiber 2g); Protein 14g

Cheesy Chicken Quesadillas

Prep Time: 25 min ▪ Start to Finish: 25 min ▪ 32 Servings (1 wedge each)

1 cup chopped cooked chicken
$1/4$ cup ranch dressing
2 teaspoons chili powder
$1/2$ teaspoon grated lime peel
4 flour tortillas (8 to 10 inch)
1 cup shredded Mexican cheese blend (4 oz)
2 medium green onions, thinly sliced (2 tablespoons)
1 tablespoon vegetable oil
Sour cream, if desired

1 Heat gas or charcoal grill. In medium bowl, mix chicken, dressing, chili powder and lime peel. Spread chicken mixture over half of each tortilla; sprinkle with cheese and onions. Fold tortilla over and press down. Brush tops with oil.

2 Place quesadillas, oil sides down, on grill. Brush tops with remaining oil. Cover grill; cook over medium-low heat 4 to 6 minutes, turning once, until both sides are golden brown and cheese is melted. Cut each into 8 wedges. Serve with sour cream.

The easy way to get cooked chicken? Buy a cooked chicken breast at the deli, and remove the skin and bones. This will give you about 1 cup of cooked chicken.

1 Serving: Calories 50 (Calories from Fat 30); Total Fat 3g (Saturated Fat 1g); Cholesterol 10mg; Sodium 70mg; Total Carbohydrate 3g (Dietary Fiber 0g; Protein 3g

Chicken Tostadas

Prep Time: 15 min ■ Start to Finish: 15 min ■ 6 Tostadas

6 tostada shells (6 inch)
1 can (15 to 16 oz) refried beans
3 cups shredded or bite-size pieces lettuce
1 1/2 cups cut-up cooked chicken or turkey
1 cup salsa
1 medium avocado, sliced
Lemon juice
3/4 cup shredded Monterey Jack or Cheddar cheese (3 oz)
2 medium tomatoes, sliced
Sour cream, if desired
Salsa, if desired

1 Heat tostada shells as directed on package. Heat beans in 1-quart saucepan over medium heat, stirring occasionally, until hot. Spread over tostada shells, sprinkle with lettuce.

2 Mix chicken and 1 cup salsa in 2-quart saucepan; heat until hot. Sprinkle avocado with lemon juice.

3 Spread chicken mixture over tostada shells. Sprinkle with cheese. Top with tomatoes and avocado. Serve with sour cream and additional salsa.

Take it easy — let folks make their own tostadas, just the way they want them.

1 Serving: Calories 325 (Calories from Fat 155); Total Fat 17g (Saturated Fat 6g); Cholesterol 50mg; Sodium 540mg; Total Carbohydrate 32g (Dietary Fiber 9g); Protein 20g

Chorizo Burritos

Prep Time: 20 min ▪ Start to Finish: 20 min ▪ 8 Servings

1 lb bulk chorizo sausage or ground beef
$1/4$ cup taco sauce
1 cup canned refried beans
8 flour tortillas (8 to 10 inch), warmed
2 cups shredded lettuce
2 medium tomatoes, chopped ($1^1/_2$ cups)
1 cup shredded taco-seasoned cheese or Cheddar cheese (4 oz)

1 Cook sausage in 10-inch skillet over medium heat, stirring occasionally, until no longer pink; drain. Stir in taco sauce and beans; reduce heat. Simmer uncovered 5 minutes.

2 Spoon about $1/4$ cup of the sausage mixture onto center of each tortilla. Top with $1/4$ cup of the lettuce and about 2 tablespoons each of the tomatoes and cheese.

3 Fold tortilla over filling.

Buy shredded cheese — it really cuts down on prep time.

1 Serving: Calories 550 (Calories from Fat 290); Total Fat 32g (Saturated Fat 12g); Cholesterol 65mg; Sodium 1230mg; Total Carbohydrate 45g (Dietary Fiber 5g); Protein 25g

Salsa-Rice Burritos

Prep Time: 15 min ▪ Start to Finish: 20 min ▪ 8 Burritos

1 1/2 cups salsa

1 1/2 teaspoons chili powder

1 cup uncooked instant rice

1 can (15 to 16 oz) black beans, drained, rinsed

1 can (11 oz) whole kernel corn with red and green peppers, undrained

1 1/2 cups shredded Cheddar cheese (6 oz)

8 flour tortillas (8 inch)

Additional salsa, if desired

1 In 10-inch skillet, heat 1 1/2 cups salsa and the chili powder to boiling. Stir in rice; remove from heat. Cover; let stand 5 minutes.

2 Stir beans, corn and cheese into rice mixture.

3 Onto center of each tortilla, spoon about 1/2 cup rice mixture. Roll tortillas around filling. Serve with additional salsa.

1 Burrito: Calories 390 (Calories from Fat 100); Total Fat 11g (Saturated Fat 5g); Cholesterol 20mg; Sodium 680mg; Total Carbohydrate 58g (Dietary Fiber 6g); Protein 16g

South-of-the-Border Burritos

Prep Time: 20 min ▪ Start to Finish: 20 min ▪ 4 Servings

2 tablespoons vegetable oil
1 large onion, chopped (1 cup)
6 cloves garlic, finely chopped
1 can (15 to 16 oz) black beans, rinsed, drained and mashed
1 to 2 teaspoons finely chopped drained chipotle chiles in adobo sauce
(from 7-oz can)
4 flour tortillas (8 or 10 inch)
1 cup shredded mozzarella cheese (4 oz)
1 large tomato, chopped (1 cup)

1 In 10-inch nonstick skillet, heat oil over medium-high heat. Cook onion and garlic in oil 6 to 8 minutes, stirring occasionally, until onion is tender. Stir in beans and chiles. Cook, stirring frequently, until hot.

2 Place one-fourth of the bean mixture on center of each tortilla. Top with cheese and tomato.

3 Fold one end of tortilla up about 1 inch over filling; fold right and left sides over folded end, overlapping. Fold remaining end down. Place seam side down on serving platter or plate.

Use a garlic press to quickly crush the garlic instead of chopping it — look for the self-cleaning type; it presses all the garlic through the holes instead of leaving the pieces behind.

1 Serving: Calories 470 (Calories from Fat 150); Total Fat 16g (Saturated Fat 6g); Cholesterol 15mg; Sodium 780mg; Total Carbohydrate 60g (Dietary Fiber 9g); Protein 21g

Grilled Fish Tacos

Prep Time: 20 min ▪ Start to Finish: 20 min ▪ 8 Tacos

1 lb medium-firm white fish fillets, such as sea bass or red snapper
1 tablespoon olive or vegetable oil
1 teaspoon ground cumin or chili powder
$^1/_2$ teaspoon salt
$^1/_4$ teaspoon pepper
8 corn tortillas (6 inch)
$^1/_4$ cup sour cream
Toppers (shredded lettuce, chopped avocado, chopped tomatoes,
     chopped onion and chopped fresh cilantro), if desired
$^1/_2$ cup salsa
Fresh lime wedges, if desired

1 Brush grill rack with vegetable oil. Heat coals or gas grill for direct heat.

2 Brush fish with oil; sprinkle with cumin, salt and pepper. Cover and grill fish over medium heat 5 to 7 minutes, turning once, until fish flakes easily with fork.

3 Heat tortillas as directed on bag. Spread sour cream on tortillas. Add fish, Toppers and salsa. Squeeze juice from lime wedges over tacos.

1 Taco: Calories 140 (Calories from Fat 40); Total Fat 4.5g (Saturated Fat 1.5g); Cholesterol 35mg; Sodium 310mg; Total Carbohydrate 12g (Dietary Fiber 2g); Protein 12g

Turkey Soft Tacos

Prep Time: 20 min ▪ Start to Finish: 20 min ▪ 4 Servings

$^1/_2$ cup chicken broth
1 medium onion, chopped ($^1/_2$ cup)
1 small red or green bell pepper, diced ($^1/_2$ cup)
$^1/_2$ cup frozen whole kernel corn (from 1-lb bag)
$^1/_2$ lb ground turkey breast
4 cloves garlic, finely chopped
$^1/_2$ cup salsa
$^1/_4$ cup chopped fresh cilantro
8 flour tortillas (8 to 10 inch), warmed*
Sour cream, if desired

1 In 10-inch nonstick skillet, heat broth to boiling over high heat. Cook onion, bell pepper and corn in broth 2 to 3 minutes, stirring occasionally, until vegetables are crisp-tender. Reduce heat to medium-high.

2 Stir in turkey and garlic. Cook 2 minutes, stirring occasionally. Stir in salsa. Cook about 5 minutes, stirring occasionally, until turkey is no longer pink. Stir in cilantro.

3 Spoon slightly less than $^1/_2$ cup turkey mixture down center of each tortilla; roll up tortilla. Serve with sour cream.

*To warm tortillas, heat them in a hot ungreased skillet or griddle for 30 seconds to 1 minute. Or wrap desired number of tortillas tightly in foil and heat in 250°F oven for 15 minutes. Or place 2 tortillas at a time between dampened microwavable paper towels or sheets of microwavable plastic wrap and microwave on High for 15 to 20 seconds until warm.

1 Serving: Calories 370 (Calories from Fat 65); Total Fat 7g (Saturated Fat 2g); Cholesterol 40mg; Sodium 710mg; Total Carbohydrate 58g (Dietary Fiber 5g); Protein 23g

Three-Bean Enchilada Chili

Prep Time: 30 min ▪ Start to Finish: 30 min ▪ 5 Servings

1 tablespoon vegetable oil
1 large onion, chopped (1 cup)
1 medium green bell pepper, chopped (1 cup)
1 can (28 oz) crushed tomatoes, undrained
1 can (15 to 16 oz) pinto beans, rinsed and drained
1 can (15 to 16 oz) dark red kidney beans, rinsed and drained
1 can (15 oz) black beans, rinsed and drained
1 can (10 oz) enchilada sauce (1$^1/_4$ cups)
1 teaspoon dried oregano leaves
Tortilla chips, broken, if desired
Shredded Cheddar cheese, if desired

1 Heat oil in 3-quart saucepan over medium-high heat. Cook onion and bell pepper in oil about 5 minutes, stirring occasionally, until crisp-tender.

2 Stir in remaining ingredients except tortilla chips and cheese. Heat to boiling; reduce heat to medium-low. Simmer uncovered 10 to 15 minutes to blend flavors, stirring occasionally.

3 Sprinkle each serving with tortilla chips and cheese.

1 Serving: Calories 370 (Calories from Fat 45); Total Fat 5g (Saturated Fat 1g); Cholesterol 0mg; Sodium 1050mg; Total Carbohydrate 78g (Dietary Fiber 22g); Protein 25g

Beef Fajita Bowls

Prep Time: 30 min ▪ Start to Finish: 30 min ▪ 4 Servings

1 cup uncooked regular long-grain rice
1 lb beef boneless sirloin steak
2 tablespoons vegetable oil
1 flour tortilla (8 inch), cut into 4x$^1/_2$-inch strips
1 bag (1 lb) frozen bell pepper and onion stir-fry
$^1/_2$ cup frozen whole kernel corn
1 cup chunky-style salsa
2 tablespoons lime juice
2 tablespoons chili sauce
$^1/_2$ teaspoon ground cumin
2 tablespoons chopped fresh cilantro

1 Cook rice as directed on package. While rice is cooking, cut beef with grain into 2-inch strips; cut strips across grain into $^1/_8$-inch slices. (Beef is easier to cut if partially frozen, 30 to 60 minutes.)

2 Heat 12-inch nonstick skillet over medium-high heat. Add oil; rotate skillet to coat bottom. Cook tortilla strips in oil 1 to 2 minutes on each side, adding additional oil if necessary, until golden brown and crisp. Drain on paper towel.

3 Add beef to skillet; stir-fry over medium-high heat 4 to 5 minutes or until beef is brown; remove beef from skillet. Add frozen bell pepper mixture and corn to skillet; stir-fry 1 minute. Cover and cook 2 to 3 minutes, stirring twice, until crisp-tender. Stir in beef, salsa, lime juice, chili sauce and cumin. Cook 2 to 3 minutes, stirring occasionally, until hot. Stir in cilantro. Divide rice among 4 bowls. Top with beef mixture and tortilla strips.

1 Serving: Calories 440 (Calories from Fat 80); Total Fat 9g (Saturated Fat 2g); Cholesterol 60mg; Sodium 480mg; Total Carbohydrate 65g (Dietary Fiber 5g); Protein 30g

This all-in-one bowl meal is a fun twist on fajitas. To save even more time, top with packaged tortilla chips instead. Then reduce the amount of oil for sautéing the beef to 1 tablespoon.

Mexican Beef and Black Beans

Prep Time: 20 min ▪ Start to Finish: 20 min ▪ 4 Servings

1 lb ground beef
1 tablespoon chopped fresh parsley or 1 teaspoon parsley flakes
1 tablespoon white wine vinegar
1 teaspoon grated lime or lemon peel
1/4 teaspoon red pepper sauce
1 medium red or green bell pepper, chopped (1 cup)
4 medium green onions, thinly sliced (1/4 cup)
2 cans (15 to 16 oz each) black beans, rinsed and drained

1 Cook beef in 10-inch skillet over medium heat 8 to 10 minutes, stirring occasionally, until brown; drain.

2 Stir in remaining ingredients. Cook about 5 minutes, stirring frequently, until hot.

Forgot to thaw the ground beef? Here's an easy way around it. Remove all wrapping material, then cook as you would thawed beef, except flip the frozen block occasionally and scrape off the browned areas as it cooks.

1 Serving: Calories 495 (Calories from Fat 155); Total Fat 17g (Saturated Fat 7g); Cholesterol 65mg; Sodium 870mg; Total Carbohydrate 60g (Dietary Fiber 15g); Protein 40g

Sweet-and-Spicy Beef Fajitas

Prep Time: 10 min ▪ Start to Finish: 15 min ▪ 6 Fajitas

1¹/₂ lb beef boneless sirloin steak
1 tablespoon vegetable oil
³/₄ cup salsa
¹/₃ cup ketchup
1 to 2 tablespoons packed brown sugar
1 tablespoon Dijon mustard
6 flour tortillas (8 inch)
Sour cream, if desired
Shredded lettuce, if desired
Chopped tomato, if desired

1 Cut beef into beef strips. (Beef is easier to cut if partially frozen, about 1¹/₂ hours.)

2 Heat 12-inch skillet or wok over high heat. Add oil; rotate skillet to coat side.

3 Add beef; stir-fry 2 to 3 minutes or until golden brown; drain. Stir in salsa, ketchup, brown sugar and mustard. Cook and stir 1 to 2 minutes or until hot. Serve in tortillas with remaining ingredients.

Look for red and green southwestern-style tortillas near the deli or in the Mexican-foods aisle of the supermarket. These colorful wraps will give your fajitas a festive look!

1 Fajita: Calories 330 (Calories from Fat 90); Total Fat 10g (Saturated Fat 3g); Cholesterol 60mg; Sodium 760mg; Total Carbohydrate 35g (Dietary Fiber 2g); Protein 27g

Fajita Pizza

Prep Time: 20 min ▪ Start to Finish: 30 min ▪ 6 Servings

2 tablespoons vegetable oil
1/2 lb boneless skinless chicken breasts, cut into 1/8- to 1/4-inch strips
1/2 medium bell pepper, cut into thin strips
1 small onion, sliced
1/2 cup salsa or picante sauce
1 1/2 cups Original Bisquick mix
1/3 cup very hot water
1 1/2 cups shredded mozzarella cheese (6 oz)

1 Move oven rack to lowest position. Heat oven to 450°F. Grease 12-inch pizza pan with shortening or butter. Heat 10-inch skillet over medium-high heat. Add oil; rotate skillet to coat bottom and side. Cook chicken in oil 3 minutes, stirring frequently. Stir in bell pepper and onion. Cook 3 to 4 minutes, stirring frequently, until vegetables are crisp and chicken is no longer pink in center; remove from heat. Stir in salsa; set aside.

2 In another bowl stir together Bisquick and very hot water until soft dough forms; beat vigorously with spoon 20 strokes. Press dough in pizza pan, using fingers dipped in Bisquick; pinch edge to form 1/2-inch rim. Sprinkle 3/4 cup of the cheese over crust. Top with chicken mixture. Sprinkle with remaining 3/4 cup cheese.

3 Bake about 12 minutes or until crust is brown and cheese is melted and bubbly.

1 Serving: Calories 295 (Calories from Fat 135); Total Fat 15g (Saturated Fat 5g); Cholesterol 40mg; Sodium 690mg; Total Carbohydrate 22g (Dietary Fiber 1g); Protein 19g

Mushroom-Pepper Whole Wheat Sandwiches

Italian Vegetable Focaccia Sandwich

Caesar Salad Wraps

California Black Bean Burgers

Cheesy Soy Burgers

Mou Shu Vegetables with Asian Pancakes

Southwestern Potato Patties

Fresh Spinach and New Potato Frittata

Chunky Vegetable Chili

Vegetable Paella

Vegetable Curry with Couscous

Scandinavian Vegetable Stew

Spicy Vegetable Stir-Fry

Edamame Stir-Fry

Tofu-Teriyaki-Mushroom Noodles

Garden Vegetable Spaghetti

Chipotle-Peanut Noodle Bowls

Spaetzle in Herbed Tomato Cream Sauce

6

make it meatless

Mushroom-Pepper Whole Wheat Sandwiches

Prep Time: 30 min ▪ Start to Finish: 30 min ▪ 4 Sandwiches

4 medium fresh portabella mushroom caps (3½ to 4 inch)
4 slices red onion, ½ inch thick
2 tablespoons reduced-fat mayonnaise or salad dressing
2 teaspoons reduced-fat balsamic vinaigrette
8 slices whole wheat bread
4 slices (¾ oz each) reduced-fat mozzarella cheese
8 strips (2x1 inch) roasted red bell pepper (from 7-oz jar), patted dry
8 large basil leaves

1 Heat closed medium-size contact grill for 5 minutes.

2 Place mushrooms on grill. Close grill; cook 4 to 5 minutes or until slightly softened. Remove mushrooms from grill. Place onion on grill. Close grill; cook 4 to 5 minutes or until slightly softened. Remove onion from grill.

3 In small bowl, mix mayonnaise and vinaigrette; spread over bread slices. Top 4 bread slices with mushrooms, cheese, onion, bell pepper and basil. Top with remaining bread, mayonnaise sides down.

4 Place 2 sandwiches on grill. Close grill; cook 2 to 3 minutes or until sandwiches are golden brown and toasted. Repeat with remaining 2 sandwiches.

1 Sandwich: Calories 260 (Calories from Fat 80); Total Fat 9g (Saturated Fat 3g); Cholesterol 10mg; Sodium 440mg; Total Carbohydrate 32g (Dietary Fiber 5g); Protein 14g

Don't let your grill gather dust on the counter — make these fast and utterly delicious sandwiches!

Italian Vegetable Focaccia Sandwich

Prep Time: 5 min ▪ Start to Finish: 5 min ▪ 6 Servings

1 round focaccia bread (10 to 12 inch)
2 cups shredded mozzarella cheese (8 oz)
2 cups deli marinated Italian vegetable salad, drained and coarsely chopped

1 Cut focaccia vertically in half, then horizontally in half. Sprinkle bottom halves of focaccia with 1 cup of the cheese. Spread vegetables over cheese. Sprinkle with remaining cheese.

2 Top with tops of bread. Cut each half into 3 wedges.

This easy sandwich filling is great in crusty Italian or French rolls as well — and makes the sandwiches more portable. Slice off the top of each roll, and remove half of the soft bread from inside. Layer the cheese and vegetable salad inside the rolls.

1 Serving: Calories 340 (Calories from Fat 145); Total Fat 16g (Saturated Fat 6g); Cholesterol 55mg; Sodium 960mg; Total Carbohydrate 33g (Dietary Fiber 2g); Protein 18g

Caesar Salad Wraps

Prep Time: 35 min ▪ Start to Finish: 35 min ▪ 4 Wraps

4 eggs
16 small romaine lettuce leaves
¼ cup chopped red onion
2 tablespoons shredded Parmesan or Romano cheese
¼ cup Caesar dressing
4 garden vegetable–flavored flour tortillas (6 to 8 inch)
2 plum (Roma) tomatoes, sliced

1 In 2-quart saucepan, place eggs in single layer; add enough cold water to cover eggs by 1 inch. Cover; heat to boiling. Remove from heat; let stand covered 15 minutes. Drain. Immediately place eggs in cold water with ice cubes or run cold water over eggs until completely cooled.

2 Meanwhile, in large bowl, toss lettuce, onion, cheese and dressing to coat. Place lettuce mixture evenly down center of each tortilla. Top with tomatoes.

3 To remove shell from each egg, crackle it by tapping gently all over; roll between hands to loosen. Peel, starting at large end. Cut eggs into slices; place over lettuce mixture with tomatoes.

4 Fold up one end of each tortilla up about 1 inch over filling; fold right and left sides over folded end, overlapping. Fold remaining end down; secure with toothpick if necessary.

1 Wrap: Calories 330 (Calories from Fat 160); Total Fat 18g (Saturated Fat 4.5g); Cholesterol 215mg; Sodium 490mg; Total Carbohydrate 29g (Dietary Fiber 2g); Protein 12g

California Black Bean Burgers

Prep Time: 25 min ▪ Start to Finish: 25 min ▪ 6 Sandwiches

1 can (15 to 16 oz) black beans, undrained
1 can (4.5 oz) chopped green chiles, undrained
1 cup plain dry bread crumbs
1 teaspoon chili powder
1 large egg, beaten
¼ cup yellow cornmeal
2 tablespoons vegetable oil
6 hamburger buns, toasted
2 tablespoons mayonnaise or salad dressing
1¼ cups shredded lettuce
3 tablespoons chunky-style salsa

1 In food processor or blender, place beans. Cover and process until slightly mashed; remove from food processor to medium bowl. Stir chiles, bread crumbs, chili powder and egg into beans. Shape mixture into 6 patties, each about ½ inch thick. Coat each patty with cornmeal.

2 In 10-inch skillet, heat oil over medium heat. Cook patties in oil 5 to 10 minutes, turning once, until crisp and thoroughly cooked on both sides.

3 Spread bottom halves of buns with mayonnaise. Top with lettuce, patties, salsa and tops of buns.

No one will miss the beef with these yummy burgers!

1 Sandwich: Calories 400 (Calories from Fat 100); Total Fat 11g (Saturated Fat 2g); Cholesterol 35mg; Sodium 1090mg; Total Carbohydrate 60g (Dietary Fiber 7g); Protein 14g

Cheesy Soy Burgers

Prep Time: 25 min ■ Start to Finish: 25 min ■ 4 Servings

Horseradish Sauce
1/2 cup plain fat-free yogurt
2 teaspoons prepared horseradish

Patties
1 can (15 or 16 oz) soybeans, drained,
    rinsed
1/2 cup shredded reduced-fat
    Cheddar cheese (2 oz)
1/4 cup unseasoned dry bread crumbs
2 medium green onions, finely
    chopped (2 tablespoons)

1 teaspoon Worcestershire sauce
1/2 teaspoon pepper
1/8 teaspoon salt
2 tablespoons fat-free egg product
    or 1 egg white

Buns
4 burger buns, split, toasted

Toppings
4 slices tomato
4 lettuce leaves

1 In small bowl, mix sauce ingredients; set aside.

2 In medium bowl, mash beans with fork. Stir in remaining patty ingredients. Shape mixture into 4 patties.

3 Spray 10-inch nonstick skillet with cooking spray. Cook patties in skillet over medium heat about 10 minutes, turning once, until light brown.

4 Top bottom halves of buns with patties, sauce, tomato and lettuce. Cover with top halves of buns.

You can use canned, drained and rinsed pinto beans here, instead of the soybeans, if you like.

1 Serving: Calories 380 (Calories from Fat 110); Total Fat 12g (Saturated Fat 2.5g); Cholesterol 0mg; Sodium 790mg; Total Carbohydrate 41g (Dietary Fiber 7g); Protein 26g

Mou Shu Vegetables with Asian Pancakes

Prep Time: 30 min ▪ Start to Finish: 30 min ▪ 6 Servings (2 pancakes each)

1 tablespoon vegetable oil
1 bag (16 oz) coleslaw mix
1 cup canned drained bean sprouts or 1 bag (8 oz) fresh bean sprouts
1 package (8 oz) sliced mushrooms (3 cups)
1 tablespoon grated gingerroot
3 tablespoons hoisin sauce
1¼ cups Original Bisquick mix
1¼ cups milk
1 egg
8 green onions, chopped (½ cup)
Additional hoisin sauce, if desired

1 Heat oil in 4-quart Dutch oven over medium-high heat. Cook coleslaw mix, bean sprouts, mushrooms and gingerroot in oil about 10 minutes, stirring frequently, until vegetables are tender. Stir in 3 tablespoons hoisin sauce. Reduce heat; keep warm.

2 Beat Bisquick mix, milk and egg in medium bowl with wire whisk or hand beater until well blended. Stir in onions. Spray 10-inch skillet with cooking spray; heat over medium-high heat. For each pancake, pour slightly less than ¼ cup batter into skillet; rotate skillet to make a thin pancake, 5 to 6 inches in diameter. Cook until bubbles break on surface; turn. Cook other side until golden brown. Keep warm while making remaining pancakes.

3 Spoon about ⅓ cup vegetable mixture onto each pancake; roll up. Serve with additional hoisin sauce.

1 Serving: Calories 225 (Calories from Fat 80); Total Fat 9g (Saturated Fat 2g); Cholesterol 40mg; Sodium 540mg; Total Carbohydrate 30g (Dietary Fiber 3g); Protein 9g

Southwestern Potato Patties

Prep Time: 10 min ▪ Start to Finish: 25 min ▪ 6 Servings

1 bag (20 oz) refrigerated Southwest-style shredded hash brown potatoes
3 eggs, beaten, or ³/₄ cup fat-free egg product
1 cup shredded reduced-fat Cheddar cheese (4 oz)
¹/₂ cup Original Bisquick mix
¹/₄ cup canola or olive oil
1 can (11 oz) whole kernel corn with red and green peppers, drained
1 can (15 to 16 oz) black beans, rinsed, drained
¹/₄ cup chunky style salsa

1 In large bowl, mix potatoes, eggs, cheese and Bisquick mix.

2 In 12-inch skillet, heat 2 tablespoons of the oil over medium heat. For each patty, spoon about ¹/₂ cup potato mixture into oil in skillet. Flatten with the back of spatula.

3 Cook patties about 4 minutes, turning once, until golden brown. Remove from skillet and cover to keep warm while cooking remaining patties. Add remaining 2 tablespoons oil as needed to prevent sticking.

4 In 2-quart saucepan, heat corn, beans and salsa over medium heat 2 to 3 minutes, stirring occasionally, until hot. Serve over patties.

1 Serving: Calories 420 (Calories from Fat 140); Total Fat 15g (Saturated Fat 3g); Cholesterol 110mg; Sodium 670mg; Total Carbohydrate 59g (Dietary Fiber 8g); Protein 17g

Fresh Spinach and New Potato Frittata

Prep Time: 30 min ▪ Start to Finish: 30 min ▪ 4 Servings

6 eggs
2 tablespoons milk
$1/4$ teaspoon dried marjoram leaves
$1/4$ teaspoon salt
2 tablespoons butter or margarine
1 lb small red potatoes (6 or 7), thinly sliced (2 cups)
$1/4$ teaspoon salt
1 cup firmly packed bite-size pieces spinach
$1/4$ cup oil-packed sun-dried tomatoes, drained and sliced
3 medium green onions, cut into $1/4$-inch pieces
$1/2$ cup shredded Swiss cheese (2 oz)

1 Beat eggs, milk, marjoram and $1/4$ teaspoon salt with fork or wire whisk until well mixed; set aside. Melt butter in 10-inch nonstick skillet over medium heat. Cover and cook potatoes and $1/4$ teaspoon salt in butter about 8 minutes, stirring occasionally, until potatoes are tender.

2 Stir in spinach, tomatoes and onions. Cook, stirring occasionally, just until spinach is wilted; reduce heat to low.

3 Carefully pour egg mixture over potato mixture. Cover and cook about 6 minutes or just until top is set. Sprinkle with cheese. Cover and cook about 1 minute or until cheese is melted.

Buy prewashed and bagged spinach to speed prep for this tasty breakfast, lunch or dinner dish.

1 Serving: Calories 330 (Calories from Fat 170); Total Fat 19g (Saturated Fat 9g); Cholesterol 345mg; Sodium 500mg; Total Carbohydrate 27g (Dietary Fiber 3g); Protein 14g

Chunky Vegetable Chili

Prep Time: 10 min ▪ Start to Finish: 30 min ▪ 4 Servings

2 medium potatoes, cubed (2 cups)
1 medium onion, chopped (¹/₂ cup)
1 small yellow bell pepper, chopped (¹/₂ cup)
1 tablespoon chili powder
1 teaspoon ground cumin
1 can (28 oz) whole tomatoes, undrained
1 can (15 to 16 oz) garbanzo beans, rinsed and drained
1 can (15 to 16 oz) black beans, rinsed and drained
1 can (8 oz) tomato sauce
1 medium zucchini, cubed (1 cup)

1 Heat all ingredients except zucchini to boiling in 4-quart Dutch oven, breaking up tomatoes and stirring occasionally; reduce heat. Cover and simmer 13 minutes.

2 Stir in zucchini. Cover and simmer 5 to 7 minutes longer or until zucchini is tender.

1 Serving: Calories 410 (Calories from Fat 35); Total Fat 4g (Saturated Fat 1g); Cholesterol 0mg; Sodium 1220mg; Total Carbohydrate 90g (Dietary Fiber 21g); Protein 24g

Vegetable Paella

Prep Time: 5 min ▪ Start to Finish: 20 min ▪ 4 Servings

2 tablespoons olive or vegetable oil
2 cloves garlic, finely chopped
1 large red onion, cut into thin wedges
1 cup uncooked quick-cooking brown rice
1 cup vegetable or chicken broth
1 can (14$^1/_2$ oz) stewed tomatoes, undrained
$^1/_2$ teaspoon saffron threads, crushed
1 bag (1 lb) frozen petite peas, baby whole carrots, snow peas and
    baby cob corn (or other combination)

1 Heat oil in 12-inch nonstick skillet over medium-high heat. Cook garlic and onion in oil, stirring frequently, until onion is tender.

2 Stir in remaining ingredients. Heat to boiling; reduce heat to medium-low. Cover and cook 5 minutes, stirring occasionally; remove from heat. Let stand covered 5 minutes.

1 Serving: Calories 270 (Calories from Fat 70); Total Fat 8g (Saturated Fat 1g); Cholesterol 0mg; Sodium 600mg; Total Carbohydrate 50g (Dietary Fiber 8g); Protein 8g

Vegetable Curry with Couscous

Prep Time: 22 min ■ Start to Finish: 22 min ■ 4 Servings

1 tablespoon vegetable oil
1 medium red bell pepper, cut into thin strips
$1/4$ cup vegetable or chicken broth
1 tablespoon curry powder
1 teaspoon salt
1 bag (1 lb) frozen broccoli, carrots and cauliflower (or other combination)
$1/2$ cup raisins
$1/3$ cup chutney
2 cups hot cooked couscous or rice
$1/4$ cup chopped peanuts

1 In 12-inch skillet, heat oil over medium-high heat. Cook bell pepper in oil 4 to 5 minutes, stirring frequently, until tender.

2 Stir in broth, curry powder, salt and vegetables. Heat to boiling. Boil about 4 minutes, stirring frequently, until vegetables are crisp-tender.

3 Stir in raisins and chutney. Serve over couscous. Sprinkle with peanuts.

1 Serving: Calories 330 (Calories from Fat 80); Total Fat 9g (Saturated Fat 1.5g); Cholesterol 0mg; Sodium 730mg; Total Carbohydrate 53g (Dietary Fiber 7g); Protein 9g

Scandinavian Vegetable Stew

Prep Time: 20 min ▪ Start to Finish: 30 min ▪ 4 Servings

8 to 10 small red potatoes, cut into quarters (3 cups)
2 cups ready-to-eat baby-cut carrots
3 tablespoons butter or margarine
3 medium green onions, sliced (1/3 cup)
3 tablespoons all-purpose flour
2 cups milk
1/2 cup frozen sweet peas
3/4 teaspoon salt
1/8 teaspoon pepper
2 tablespoons chopped fresh or 1/2 teaspoon dried dill weed
1 hard-cooked egg, chopped

1 In 3-quart saucepan, place potatoes and carrots; add enough water to cover. Heat to boiling. Reduce heat to medium; cover and cook 8 to 10 minutes or until tender. Drain in colander. Wipe out saucepan with paper towel.

2 In same saucepan, melt butter over medium heat. Add onions; cook 2 minutes, stirring occasionally. Stir in flour. Gradually add milk, stirring constantly, until mixture thickens and boils.

3 Stir in potatoes and carrots, peas, salt and pepper. Cook 5 to 6 minutes, stirring occasionally, until peas are tender.

4 Stir in dill weed. Cook 2 minutes, stirring constantly. Top individual servings with chopped egg and, if desired, additional dill weed.

1 Serving: Calories 310 (Calories from Fat 110); Total Fat 13g (Saturated Fat 6g); Cholesterol 85mg; Sodium 610mg; Total Carbohydrate 39g (Dietary Fiber 5g); Protein 10g

Spicy Vegetable Stir-Fry

Prep Time: 25 min ▪ Start to Finish: 25 min ▪ 6 Servings

1 tablespoon chili or vegetable oil
2 teaspoons grated gingerroot
1 can (15 oz) whole straw mushrooms, drained
1 can (15 oz) baby corn, drained
1 can (8 oz) sliced bamboo shoots, drained
1 medium red bell pepper, cut into $1/4$-inch strips
1 cup snow pea pods
1 tablespoon finely chopped fresh cilantro
4 cups shredded Chinese (napa) cabbage (1 lb)
2 teaspoons chili puree with garlic

1 Heat wok or 12-inch skillet over high heat. Add oil; rotate wok to coat side. Add gingerroot; stir-fry 30 seconds.

2 Add mushrooms, corn, bamboo shoots, bell pepper, pea pods and cilantro; stir-fry about 2 minutes or until vegetables are crisp-tender. Stir in cabbage. Stir in chili puree; cook and stir 30 seconds.

If you don't have chili oil, you can add 1 seeded and finely chopped japaleño chile with the gingerroot.

1 Serving: Calories 115 (Calories from Fat 25); Total Fat 3g (Saturated Fat 0g); Cholesterol 0mg; Sodium 470mg; Total Carbohydrate 23g (Dietary Fiber 6g); Protein 5g

Edamame Stir-Fry

Prep Time: 15 min ▪ Start to Finish: 15 min ▪ 4 Servings

1 tablespoon vegetable oil
1 tablespoon curry powder
1 bag (1 lb) frozen stir-fry bell peppers and onions
1 bag (12 oz) frozen shelled edamame soybeans
4 cloves garlic, finely chopped
1 cup unsweetened coconut milk (not cream of coconut)
2 cups hot cooked jasmine or brown rice
$^1/_2$ cup salted roasted cashews
Chopped fresh cilantro or parsley, if desired

1 In 12-inch nonstick skillet, heat oil over medium-high heat. Cook curry powder in oil 1 minute, stirring frequently. Stir in bell peppers and onions, soybeans and garlic. Cook 2 minutes, stirring frequently. Cover and cook about 3 minutes longer or until vegetables are tender.

2 Stir in coconut milk; reduce heat. Simmer uncovered 2 minutes, stirring occasionally.

3 Serve mixture over rice. Sprinkle with cashews and cilantro.

No edamame? You can use a box (9 ounces) of frozen green peas instead.

1 Serving: Calories 560 (Calories from Fat 270); Total Fat 29g (Saturated Fat 12g); Cholesterol 0mg; Sodium 280mg; Total Carbohydrate 51g (Dietary Fiber 10g); Protein 22g

Tofu-Teriyaki-Mushroom Noodles

Prep Time: 30 min ▪ Start to Finish: 30 min ▪ 4 Servings

6 dried Chinese black or shiitake mushrooms ($^1/_2$ oz)

8 oz uncooked soba (buckwheat) noodles or whole wheat spaghetti

1 package (14 oz) firm tofu packed in water, drained

1 tablespoon vegetable oil

1 large onion, sliced

1 package (8 oz) sliced fresh mushrooms (3 cups)

8 oz fresh shiitake, crimini or baby portabella mushrooms, sliced

$^1/_3$ cup teriyaki sauce

$^1/_4$ cup chopped fresh cilantro

1 In small bowl, pour 1 cup hot water over dried mushrooms; let stand about 20 minutes or until soft.

2 Meanwhile, cook and drain noodles as directed on package. Place drained tofu between 2 layers of paper towels; press gently to remove as much water as possible. Cut into $^1/_4$-inch cubes; set aside.

3 Drain water from dried mushrooms; rinse with warm water and drain again. Squeeze out excess moisture from mushrooms. Remove and discard stems; cut caps into $^1/_2$-inch strips.

4 In 12-inch skillet or wok, heat oil over medium-high heat. Add onion; cook and stir 3 minutes. Add all mushrooms and tofu; cook and stir 3 minutes. Stir in teriyaki sauce. Reduce heat; partially cover and simmer about 2 minutes or until vegetables are tender. Stir in noodles, cilantro and, if desired, 1 tablespoon toasted sesame seed.

1 Serving: Calories 420 (Calories from Fat 90); Total Fat 10g (Saturated Fat 1.5g); Cholesterol 0mg; Sodium 1150mg; Total Carbohydrate 58g (Dietary Fiber 7g); Protein 24g

Garden Vegetable Spaghetti

Prep Time: 25 min ■ Start to Finish: 25 min ■ 6 Servings

1 package (16 oz) spaghetti
2 tablespoons olive or vegetable oil
2 medium carrots, sliced (1 cup)
1 medium onion, chopped ($^1/_2$ cup)
2 medium zucchini, cut into $^1/_2$-inch slices (4 cups)
2 cloves garlic, finely chopped
3 medium tomatoes, cut into 1-inch pieces
$^1/_2$ cup frozen green peas (from 1-lb bag), thawed
1 tablespoon chopped fresh or 1 teaspoon dried basil leaves
$^1/_2$ teaspoon salt
$^1/_4$ teaspoon pepper
$^2/_3$ cup grated Parmesan cheese

1 Cook and drain spaghetti as directed on package.

2 Meanwhile, in 10-inch skillet, heat oil over medium-high heat. Cook carrots, onion, zucchini and garlic in oil, stirring frequently, until vegetables are crisp-tender.

3 Stir in remaining ingredients except cheese; cook until hot. Serve vegetable mixture over spaghetti. Sprinkle with cheese.

1 small eggplant (about 12 ounces), peeled and diced ($3^1/_2$ cups), can be substituted for the zucchini.

1 Serving: Calories 440 (Calories from Fat 90); Total Fat 10g (Saturated Fat 3g); Cholesterol 10mg; Sodium 430mg; Total Carbohydrate 71g (Dietary Fiber 7g); Protein 17g

Chipotle-Peanut Noodle Bowls

Prep Time: 30 min ▪ Start to Finish: 30 min ▪ 4 Servings

1/2 cup creamy peanut butter
1/2 cup apple juice
2 tablespoons soy sauce
2 chipotle chilies in adobo sauce (from 7-oz can), seeded and chopped
1 teaspoon adobo sauce from can of chiles
1/4 cup chopped fresh cilantro
4 cups water
2 medium carrots, cut into julienne strips
1 medium red bell pepper, cut into julienne strips
1 package (8 to 10 oz) Chinese curly noodles
2 tablespoons chopped peanuts

1 In small bowl, mix peanut butter, apple juice, soy sauce, chiles and adobo sauce until smooth. Stir in cilantro.

2 In 2-quart saucepan, heat water to boiling. Add carrots and bell pepper; cook 1 minute. Remove carrots and bell pepper from water with slotted spoon. Add noodles to water; cook and drain as directed on package.

3 Toss noodles with peanut butter mixture; divide noodles among 4 bowls. Top with carrots and bell pepper. Sprinkle with peanuts.

1 Serving: Calories 500 (Calories from Fat 180); Total Fat 20g (Saturated Fat 4g); Cholesterol 0mg; Sodium 800mg; Total Carbohydrate 62g (Dietary Fiber 7g); Protein 18g

Spaetzle in Herbed Tomato Cream Sauce

Prep Time: 20 min ▪ Start to Finish: 20 min ▪ 4 Servings

1 teaspoon olive or vegetable oil
4 plum (Roma) tomatoes, cut into fourths and sliced (2 cups)
2 cloves garlic, finely chopped
2 tablespoons chopped fresh chives
1 tablespoon chopped fresh or 1 teaspoon dried basil leaves
$^1/_4$ cup sour cream
2 tablespoons mayonnaise or salad dressing
1 package (12 oz) frozen cooked spaetzle (4 cups)

1 Heat oil in 10-inch nonstick skillet over medium heat. Cook tomatoes and garlic in oil 5 to 7 minutes, stirring occasionally, until tomatoes are tender; reduce heat to low.

2 Stir in chives, basil, sour cream and mayonnaise. Cook 2 to 3 minutes, stirring occasionally, until sauce is hot.

3 Meanwhile, heat spaetzle as directed on package. Add hot spaetzle to skillet; toss to coat with sauce.

For an even quicker side, toss the spaetzle with warmed bottled spaghetti sauce and add $^1/_4$ cup half-and-half to make it rich and creamy.

1 Serving: Calories 110 (Calories from Fat 25); Total Fat 3g (Saturated Fat 1g); Cholesterol 50mg; Sodium 220mg; Total Carbohydrate 17g (Dietary Fiber 1g); Protein 5g

Quick Desserts

Dark Chocolate Fondue

Prep Time: 30 min
Start to Finish: 30 min
16 Servings

8 cups assorted fresh fruit
    (sliced kiwifruit, sliced bananas,
    strawberries, Bing cherries,
    cut-up pineapple, dried apricot
    halves, green grapes)
1 can (14 oz) fat-free sweetened
    condensed milk (not evaporated)
1 cup semisweet chocolate chips (6 oz)
$1/4$ cup dark chocolate syrup
$1/4$ cup boiling water
2 teaspoons instant espresso coffee
    granules
1 teaspoon vanilla

1. Prepare fruits; set aside.

2. In 2-quart saucepan, cook milk,
chocolate chips and chocolate syrup
over low heat 5 to 8 minutes, stirring
frequently, until chips are melted.

3. In small bowl, stir boiling water
and coffee granules until granules are
dissolved. Stir into chocolate mixture.
Cook over low heat 5 minutes, stirring
frequently. Stir in vanilla. Remove
from heat; pour into fondue pot.

4. Using fondue forks, dip fruit into
chocolate mixture.

Quick Praline Bars

Prep Time: 10 min
Start to Finish: 20 min
About 2 dozen bars

24 graham cracker squares
$1/2$ cup packed brown sugar
$1/2$ cup butter or margarine
$1/2$ teaspoon vanilla
$1/2$ cup chopped pecans

1. Heat oven to 350°F. Arrange
crackers in single layer in ungreased
jelly roll pan, 15 $1/2$x10$1/2$x1 inch.

2. Heat brown sugar and butter to
boiling in 2-quart saucepan. Boil 1
minute, stirring constantly; remove
from heat. Stir in vanilla.

3. Pour sugar mixture over crackers;
spread evenly. Sprinkle with pecans.
Bake 8 to 10 minutes or until bubbly;
cool slightly.

It's a snap! How about adding a quick,
    irresistible chocolate topping? Sprinkle
    $1/2$ cup semisweet chocolate chips over the
    crackers immediately after removing them
    from the oven. When completely melted,
    "spread" the chips.

Quick Rice and Raisin Pudding

Prep Time: 7 min
Start to Finish: 12 min
4 Servings

1 cup uncooked instant rice
1 cup milk or water
1/4 cup raisins
3 tablespoons sugar
1/4 teaspoon salt
1/4 teaspoon ground cinnamon or
    nutmeg

1. Mix all ingredients in 2-quart saucepan.

2. Heat to boiling, stirring constantly; remove from heat. Cover and let stand 5 minutes.

Come & eat! This pudding works with your schedule — it's delicious right out of the pan, warm, cool or chilled. Leftovers are great for breakfast too!

Blueberry-Nectarine Dessert Tortillas

Prep Time: 20 min
Start to Finish: 20 min
4 Servings

4 flour tortillas (about 7 inch)
1/2 cup semisweet chocolate chips
2 teaspoons shortening
1 cup blueberries or raspberries
3 medium nectarines or peaches, sliced
1/2 cup peach yogurt

1. Heat each tortilla in warmed skillet or microwave oven 15 to 20 seconds to soften. Press each tortilla into 10-ounce custard cup, forming a shell. Microwave uncovered on High 2 to 3 minutes, rotating cups 1/2 turn after 2 minutes, until tortillas feel dry. Remove from cups.

2. Place chocolate chips and shortening in small bowl. Microwave uncovered on High 1 to 2 minutes or until softened; stir until smooth. Dip edges of tortillas into melted chocolate. Drizzle remaining chocolate on inside of tortillas. Refrigerate about 10 minutes or until chocolate is firm.

3. Mix blueberries and nectarines; spoon into tortillas. Top with yogurt.

Helpful Nutrition and Cooking Information

Recommended intake for a daily diet of 2,000 calories as set by the Food and Drug Administration

Total Fat	Less than 65g
Saturated Fat	Less than 20g
Cholesterol	Less than 300mg
Sodium	Less than 2,400mg
Total Carbohydrate	300g
Dietary Fiber	25g

Calculating Nutrition Information

* The first ingredient is used wherever a choice is given (such as $1/3$ cup sour cream or plain yogurt).

* The first ingredient amount is used wherever a range is given (such as 2 to 3 teaspoons).

* The first serving number was used wherever a range is given (such as 4 to 6 servings).

* "If desired" ingredients and recipe variations were not included (such as sprinkle with brown sugar, if desired).

* Only the amount of a marinade or frying oil that is absorbed by the food during preparation was calculated.

Ingredients Used in Recipe Testing and Nutrition Calculations

The following ingredients, based on most commonly purchased ingredients, are used unless indicated otherwise:

* large eggs, 2% milk, 80%-lean ground beef, canned chicken broth and vegetable oil spread containing at least 65% fat when margarine is used.

* Solid vegetable shortening (not butter, margarine, or nonstick cooking spray) is used to grease pans.

Equipment Used in Recipe Testing

* Cookware and bakeware without nonstick coatings were used, unless otherwise indicated.

* No dark-colored, black or insulated bakeware was used.

* When a pan is specified, a metal pan was used; a baking dish or pie plate means ovenproof glass was used.

* An electric hand mixer was used for mixing when mixer speeds are specified.

Metric Conversion Guide

VOLUME

U.S. Units	Canadian Metric	Australian Metric
1/4 teaspoon	1 mL	1 ml
1/2 teaspoon	2 mL	2 ml
1 teaspoon	5 mL	5 ml
1 tablespoon	15 mL	20 ml
1/4 cup	50 mL	60 ml
1/3 cup	75 mL	80 ml
1/2 cup	125 mL	125 ml
2/3 cup	150 mL	170 ml
3/4 cup	175 mL	190 ml
1 cup	250 mL	250 ml
1 quart	1 liter	1 liter
1 1/2 quarts	1.5 liters	1.5 liters
2 quarts	2 liters	2 liters
2 1/2 quarts	2.5 liters	2.5 liters
3 quarts	3 liters	3 liters
4 quarts	4 liters	4 liters

WEIGHT

U.S. Units	Canadian Metric	Australian Metric
1 ounce	30 grams	30 grams
2 ounces	55 grams	60 grams
3 ounces	85 grams	90 grams
4 ounces (1/4 pound)	115 grams	125 grams
8 ounces (1/2 pound)	225 grams	225 grams
16 ounces (1 pound)	455 grams	500 grams
1 pound	455 grams	1/2 kilogram

MEASUREMENTS

Inches	Centimeters
1	2.5
2	5.0
3	7.5
4	10.0
5	12.5
6	15.0
7	17.5
8	20.5
9	23.0
10	25.5
11	28.0
12	30.5
13	33.0

TEMPERATURES

Fahrenheit	Celsius
32°	0°
212°	100°
250°	120°
275°	140°
300°	150°
325°	160°
350°	180°
375°	190°
400°	200°
425°	220°
450°	230°
475°	240°
500°	260°

NOTE: The recipes in this cookbook have not been developed or tested using metric measures. When converting recipes to metric, some variations in quality may be noted.

Index

Whatever's on the menu, make it easy with *Betty Crocker*

Betty Crocker
chicken
tonight
100 Recipes for the Way You Really Cook

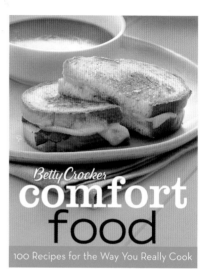

Betty Crocker
comfort
food
100 Recipes for the Way You Really Cook

Betty Crocker
party
food
100 Recipes for the Way You Really Cook

Betty Crocker
quick
fixes
100 Recipes for the Way You Really Cook